Ghost Stories of Pittsburgh
and Allegheny County

by
Beth E. Trapani
and
Charles J. Adams III

EXETER HOUSE BOOKS
1994

GHOST STORIES of
PITTSBURGH and ALLEGHENY COUNTY
©1994 Beth E. Trapani and Charles J. Adams III
Published by EXETER HOUSE BOOKS

FIRST EDITION
PRINTED IN THE UNITED STATES OF AMERICA

ISBN 1-880683-05-9

TABLE OF CONTENTS

INTRODUCTION
by Charles J. Adams III

I cringe whenever anyone asks me that one, forbidding question: *Do you believe in ghosts?*

I have given hundreds of lectures on the supernatural, and have researched and written books on ghosts and legends in the Pocono Mountains, Schuylkill Valley and Dutch Country of Pennsylvania and the capes and barrier islands of New Jersey and Delaware.

Thus, there is a general perception among those I meet that I *believe in ghosts.*

Most certainly I believe in ghosts. I believe they exist in the manner that clouds, and a summer's breeze exist.

One cannot capture a cloud or hold prisoner a breeze. If it were possible to leap thousands of feet into the sky with an open jar and seize a cirrus, it would be impossible to return to earth with absolute proof that clouds exist.

So, too, would it be folly to attempt to corral the wind.

But who can deny that both clouds and wind do truly exist? Because they cannot be retrieved and wrapped, packaged and presented for all to see does not mean they are not very real.

A device I have employed from time to time when I speak to groups is equally provocative in the attempt to illustrate the elusiveness of ghosts.

In as dramatic terms as I am able, I reveal to all present that I have "sensed" faces and voices within the walls of the room we share.

In fact, I say, these disembodied visual and audible

I

entities–unseen and unheard by the unaware audience–move freely through walls, fixtures, furniture and the bodies of everyone in the room.

After a bit of histrionics, I inform them of my regrets for having neglected to bring with me a sophisticated electronic device I own which could detect, identify and even display some of those voices and faces.

There is scarcely a time that my little ruse does not invite a puzzled response from my subjects.

Just who, they wonder, are the voices and faces that swirl invisibly among them?

Just what kind of gear could detect these supernatural signals from wherever it is that they exist?

Carefully, I reveal that those faces and voices are those which emanate not from some ethereal level, but from very real places such as the evening news, the morning radio show, and the night's ball game.

They are the invisible faces and voices of radio and television broadcasts–hundreds, if not thousands of them bombarding our bodies and zipping invisibly through our spaces.

The sophisticated electronic device which could detect and identify these stealthy visitors is a television monitor, or a radio.

As with clouds and the wind–products of nature–these broadcast signals–products of human technology–cannot be bound. Still, they all exist.

Similarly, electrical currents and magnetic fields are essentially imperceptible. Their results can be seen and felt, but their oscillations and transmissions are invisible.

And this brings the ghostly analogy into clearer focus.

The curious public has an insatiable appetite for spirits which are "evil"–ghosts said to return with a vicious vengeance and wreak havoc on their unsuspecting mortal victims.

I am met with incredulous arched eyebrows when I profess that I believe no ghost or spirit to be inherently evil.

II

I fall back on an entity as mundane as electricity to explain that belief.

Are electrical currents, in and of themselves, malevolent or benevolent? As I write this, an electrical current powers my computer, the CD player to my right and the light over my head.

I have spent an entire day enjoying the benefits of electricity. Should I be fool enough to find an empty light socket, wet my finger and plunge it into the "hot" socket, I would likely die.

Would the electricity be guilty of my death? I think not. I think that my own ignorance would have been the cause of my demise.

Such is the case with ghosts.

Ghosts, I believe, are nothing more than charges of weak electrical surges that have remained after the death of a human being.

It is medical fact that there are electrical charges in our bodies. They power our brain, our nervous system, etc. And, if it is as we were taught that matter cannot be destroyed, this matter must remain somewhere after the vessel of flesh in which it was wrapped is no longer functional.

That corporeal container, no longer coursed by the liquids, gases and impulses that gave it life, is left to disintegrate. But, the electrical charges once within it may indeed explode from that container and find their way in the open atmosphere.

Could it be that those charges remains, still virtually intact, and somehow finds a host upon which it resides, or more properly, records itself?

If there is any one common thread which runs through nearly every story I have ever investigated, it is that the "ghostly" activity nearly always coincides with recent or active renovations within the afflicted "haunted house."

Walls have been removed, window frames replaced, roofs repaired, floors redone. Whether the afflicted individual, couple or family knew it or not, the spectral sensations were strangely timed with these work projects.

There are those far more schooled in the sciences than I who believe that the "host" of this leftover energy from a human life could well be rust.

Rust.

It is not entirely inconceivable that rust may indeed be the key to the understanding of ghostly sightings, sounds and sensations.

Some say the electrical energy–the "ghost"–imprints itself on rusty surfaces in much the same way sound and light waves and vibrations record themselves on video and audio tape.

The waves and vibrations are undetectable to the eye, as is the product on the raw tape. Played back on a special machine, however, they become vividly evident.

In the case of ghosts, that "playback" mechanism is the medium or psychic who can tune in to the energy which has been deposited on rusty surfaces.

When those rusty surfaces are disturbed, or exposed after a long period of time, they then release their information to those with sensitive minds.

This leads to the answer to another question I am asked many times: Why is it that some people have the ability to see or hear ghosts, while others do not?

I think every one of us has that capability, just as every one of us with two arms, a brain and a chin is capable of playing the violin. Each of us is capable of hitting a home run off a major league pitcher. Each of us is capable of singing in an opera.

However, if we never pick up a violin or a baseball bat, or never take voice lessons, we will never know of those abilities. What might have been the greatest high jumper the world has ever known may never have jumped out of fear, disinterest or distraction.

Some people fear the notion of encountering a ghost, and brace themselves psychically against that possibility.

Some people deny the existence of ghosts and summarily dismiss the notion.

However, some people welcome that same notion and hone their psychic skills to accept the energy into their lives and minds.

Coupled with a bit of historical investigation and documentation and one other valuable human trait, those shards of information from that cold, emotionless energy are converted into fates, forms and features.

That other human trait is every bit as important to the understanding of things ghostly as the physical and metaphysical elements.

That trait is the imagination.

While it is not to be implied that ghosts are the product of the imagination, it is allowed by even the most serious investigator of the paranormal that the imagination does play a role in the refinement of the senses and sciences that emerges from the psyche as a "ghost."

It is the imagination which clothes and animates that shard of psychic evidence. It is the imagination which converts innocuous nocturnal sounds into "things that go bump in the night."

Yes, ghosts exist. They are a part of every culture, they recur through every period of time in history, and they are pivotal players in every form of literature, music and art.

What's more, they are all around you. As you will read in the following pages, ghosts have been detected in places you may go by people you may know.

These are the ghost stories of Pittsburgh and Allegheny County.

As a native of eastern Pennsylvania, I have always looked at Pittsburgh as a faraway place on the other side of the mountains.

My visits to Pittsburgh had been short and cordial over the course of my life. Only in the research stage of compiling this book have I learned to more fully understand the city and the county which surrounds it.

V

Pittsburgh is still over the mountains and fairly far away from my Berks County home. But, its geography, its history, its vibrancy–and especially its people–have endeared themselves to this individual who has spent a lifetime knowing more the Delaware, Lehigh and Schuylkill than the Monongahela, Allegheny and Ohio; the Poconos rather than the Laurels; Mr. Penn versus Mr. Pitt and–forgive me this–the Eagles and Nittany Lions instead of the Steelers and Panthers.

It was the young woman who actually wrote every word you are about to read who lured me to participate in the publication of a book about the ghost stories of Pittsburgh.

As a freshman at Carnegie Mellon University–with already impressive writing credentials–Beth saw beyond what most people see when they are transplanted to a city or region.

Herself a native of the other side of the mountains which split the Commonwealth, she plunged into the folklore, the legends and onto the dim trails of dark tales which run parallel to the mainstream avenues of history.

Beth Trapani wandered on those unmarked trails and urged me to follow. Along the way, our passage was brightened by countless guides, and at the end of the long journey was this book.

I thank Beth for asking me to accompany her. I thank you for tagging along for the next few hours.

Pittsburgh is a city with a long and proud heritage, a dynamic present and a secure future.

As I write this from a room high in a downtown hotel, I look out my window and am treated to a sweeping panorama of this exciting city.

The longer I survey the cityscape, the more I am reminded of a wildly different but hauntingly similar vista I enjoyed on a recent trip abroad.

If the mighty rivers of Pittsburgh were *wadi*–the dry river bed ravines of Israel–instead of watery avenues of commerce and trade, Pittsburgh could pass as Jerusalem.

If the hills of the city were arid and tan rather than lush and green, they could serve as the Judean Hills.

As Jerusalem is the gateway to the Middle East, Pittsburgh is the gateway to America's Middle West.

As Jerusalem is the crossroads of cultures, Pittsburgh is, as well.

Consider Mt. Washington as the Mount of Olives. Instead of a view from there of the holy shrines of the world's great spiritual powers, it affords a view of the towers of economic and educational powers.

But at once, intermingled on the hillocks and plains which stretch beyond these glitzy, glassy skyscrapers, are the no less important spires of the many religions represented by the people of Pittsburgh.

As Jerusalem is divided into distinct cultural enclaves, Pittsburgh's neighborhoods–while less clearly defined–also retain the legends and folklore of those immigrants who settled them.

From the Germanic flavor of the North Side to the Slavic and Ukraine neighborhoods of the South Side to the obvious ethnic roots of Polish Hill, Pittsburgh is a salad bowl of cultures.

Every one of those cultures has its foods, its music, its dress, its art, its religion, its language, and its representation of the supernatural.

This book is not intended to be an historical treatise or a ponderous probe of the paranormal.

Its intent was and is to gather the ghost stories of real people at real places in a most real city and county.

Pittsburgh is a bright and vibrant place to visit, work or reside.

In this book, we leave that brilliance and go to a place where the lights are dim, all is quiet, all is just right for a few good, old fashioned ghost stories.

Sleep tight tonight!

Charles J. Adams III
Pittsburgh, Pennsylvania
July, 1994

VII

UNCLE VICTOR'S APOLOGY

The "unfinished business" theory has brought back the spirits of countless loved ones. Some say a soul cannot rest until it has attended to pending matters or fulfilled a duty and cleared its conscience.

For one North Side specter, death was no obstacle to an apology.

"It was several years ago, probably ten or more," said Heather, a young woman captivated by her family's story.

"My mother was in a Catholic church with my father's Aunt Mary. The women were walking down a side aisle when my Aunt Mary stopped to light a candle for her dead husband, Victor."

It is the waxing of this flame that will illuminate the family's tale.

During their marriage, Victor and Mary occupied a North Side row home. According to Heather, the union was wracked with instability, due in large part to Victor's alcoholism. A devout Catholic, Mary refused to request a divorce, however, and the two remained a couple until Victor's death in 1978.

Mary married shortly thereafter, this time to a man named Frank. About two months into the marriage, the new couple decided to move to Mt. Lebanon and rent out the row home.

A young mother with a baby moved into the home, finding the space all ready occupied.

Apparently, Uncle Victor had not left the premises!

1

"One night, sometime close to Christmas, the woman carried the baby upstairs to the bedroom," said Heather. "She finished tucking in the baby and turned to head down the stairs. There were no lights on downstairs, only the light of the street lights through the curtains.

"She looked down the stairs and saw a man standing in the hallway by the living room doorway. She asked him if she could help him, or what he wanted. He said nothing, turned, and walked into the dining room. At that point, I think I would have ran!"

Bolstering her courage, the woman, determined to discover what the stranger was doing in her home, made her way slowly down the stairs, through the dining room and into the kitchen. She found nothing but tightly secured doors.

"I guess he must have looked a tad transparent," said Heather, "because she called my aunt that night and told her what happened. When my aunt asked what he looked like, the young woman described my Uncle Victor to a tee."

Unnerved by her renter's experience, Mary lit a candle to pray for rest for Victor's soul and asked a priest to bless the house.

Nothing more was heard of Victor for two years.

Again, on a late December evening, the woman tucked her child in for the night, and went downstairs to watch TV.

A few moments later, she heard her daughter call, "Mommy, Mommy, come upstairs and meet the nice man!"

Alarmed, the woman rushed to the bottom of the staircase where a revealing view of her daughter's room caused her to stop, cold. Kneeling beside the child's bed was what appeared to be a man.

The woman slowly began the ascent, shocked and concerned by the visitation. As she climbed, the figure rose, walked to a corner of the bedroom and disappeared.

Heather matter-of-factly relayed the story. "Yep, she saw my Uncle Victor play with her daughter and disappear in the corner."

"When I heard about the second sighting, I said to my mother, 'It sounds like Uncle Victor is trying to find Aunt Mary. Maybe he just wants to apologize for the way he treated her.'

"About a night or two later, Uncle Victor's daughter, Caroline, who was grown with children of her own, was sound asleep and had a very vivid dream. She said in her dream, Victor walked into her bedroom, looked down at her and said, 'Where is your mother? I cannot find your Mother.'

"Caroline told him that Mary no longer lived in the house, and that she had remarried and was very happy.

"With that he disappeared and no one in the family or house has seen him since."

Perhaps Uncle Victor found his rest.

•

GREENFIELD'S GHOSTLY GUEST

Pittsburgh's municipal resume boasts a lengthy list of "Quality of Life" awards.

In 1985, Pittsburgh was named Most Livable City in the United States by *Rand McNally's Places Rated Almanac*. Since then, it has garnered a number of similar awards and enough positive attention to position the "steel city," the "smoky city," atop the list of nationally recognized great places to live and work. No question, the 'Burgh is in.

At least one visitor to the city liked the place well enough to stick around, echoing the words of Thomas Wolfe, "You Can't Go Home Again."

Apparently, a Lancaster County, Pennsylvania man cannot return to his bucolic, eastern Pennsylvania home.

Nancy, a Greenfield resident and mother of three, said her father-in-law, Jim, was visiting from Lancaster County the day after Thanksgiving, 1986, when he fell ill.

"He thought he was getting sick in his stomach," recalled Nancy. "He went upstairs and laid down in our back bedroom, which is the guest room. He ate lunch later, around two in the afternoon, and afterwards nearly passed out on the stairs. I helped carry him to bed, and he was absolutely white.

"His eyes were open and he was staring through us. He wasn't looking *at* me, but *through* me. I was screaming his name, but he wasn't answering me. Finally he said, 'Nancy!'

"I said, 'Why didn't you answer me?'

"He said, 'I could hear you, but all I could see was a

4

bright light.'

"I was very shaken by this, and begged him to let me call an ambulance. He wouldn't let me. He had very strong convictions about the afterlife, and I think he knew what was going to happen."

Jim died of heart failure later that day in the back bedroom of the small, three-bedroom home. Nancy, her husband, their children, and Jim's wife traveled to Lancaster County the next day to attend to funeral arrangements and to spend time with Jim's wife in her home.

"After Jim's death, we had been away from the house for a period of three or four days," said Nancy. "A friend, Mark, who always stayed in the house to watch the cats and things like that was staying in it again while we were away. He hadn't called us to tell us about any problems, but he did leave us a note that said he couldn't get into the back bedroom (the guest room) where he usually slept, so he slept in our bedroom. When I read the note, I went upstairs and tried opening the door. The knob would turn, but the bedside table was directly in front of the door and door jamb and there was a lamp sitting on the table!

"The table normally sat to the left of the door jamb beside the bed, but somehow it had been moved a good eight inches to the right and the lamp was still there on it. There's no way that could have happened...I was absolutely flipping out!

Struck by the realization that the redecorator worked from the inside of the room, Nancy was anxious to inspect the area for signs of intruders.

"I managed to get my hand in the door, knocked the lamp onto the bed and managed to move the table," she said. "The room was fine–nothing was touched besides the table and lamp. Since it was wintertime, all the windows were secured. No one could have moved that table in front of the door like that, especially since the lamp was left on it."

Baffled by the achievement of the seeming physical

impossibility, Nancy's blame soon fell on dear and familiar shoulders.

She believes Jim was responsible for the obstruction, and said even her oft-skeptical husband thinks his father may well be the one who blocked the door.

"We thought the fact that Mark was staying in the house had something to do with it," said Nancy. "He's not a member of the family, and maybe Jim barricaded the door because he didn't want to be disturbed by him."

Nancy thinks she found other vestiges of Jim about the house.

Perhaps her cat, Sammy, did as well. The animal that never before set paw in the bedroom sprayed the room shortly after Jim's death, causing damage so extensive that Nancy was forced to replace an area of the carpet where the feline left its mark.

A different kind of aroma could be found in the room as well.

"I distinctly remember a smell in that room," said Nancy. "You know when someone stayed in your house and you smell them or their cologne? Well, that's what this was. After we got back from Lancaster County and I went back into the room I opened all the windows and let the doors open for a while. I thought maybe someone was trying to get out."

According to Nancy, the scent of cologne never dissipated, even after several fervent attempts to rid the room of it. "For as much as I aired the room out, it never went away," she said.

"But things like this don't scare me. I think it's a form of communication."

Nancy and her family moved to another Pittsburgh suburb 15 months later. "We moved in part to sever all of this. It never bothered me, but we felt that maybe Jim isn't at peace. I think he knew there was an afterlife, and he believed in forms of reincarnation."

Ironically, a death in the family occurred shortly

6

before the birth of each of Nancy's children. In fact, Nancy is nearly certain of the conception date of her second child, a day also marked by the death of her grandmother.

Do these "coincidences" lead Nancy to believe reincarnation may be at work in her family?

"You can't dwell on stuff like that because it would drive you nuts, but on the other hand, I'm one of those people who isn't scared of it. We'll never really know...

"I used to get bugged. I'd think, 'Now I'm in bed with my husband, is Jim watching?' But, if spirits are beyond this complete human state, then they understand humanness.

"I believe the afterlife is all around us. There are forces that we just don't see."

And there are guests who just don't leave.

•

CLAYTON:
HOME OF GHOSTLY CHARM

It was a dark and stormy night.

Well, not exactly.

But it was at least a close daytime approximation of that infamous setting when we arrived at The Frick Art & Historical Center.

The damp chill of the harsh winter day made its breath-constricting presence known as we walked through the ornate iron gates of the estate.

A brace of black crows circled in the steel gray sky as we passed the low, marble grave markers where Frick family pets lie.

A feeling of anticipation descended upon us as Clayton, the expansive, turn-of-the-century mansion rose before us.

There, within feet, stood a ghost hunter's Utopia.

In the classic sense of Victoriana, the place looks haunted.

The spiny fingers of tree branches laid bare by the season directed all attention to Clayton. We were engulfed in the rush of the anachronistic experience the Frick estate provides and exchanged now-familiar glances that said, "It has to be haunted."

The annals of Clayton and the Frick Art & Historical Center are an intricate component of the supernatural story with which we were concerned.

A stop in the Visitors Center provided detailed insight

8

to the estate's well-documented past.

Industrial magnate Henry Clay Frick married Adelaide Howard Childs on December 15, 1881. The following summer, the Fricks paid $25,000 for 1.5 acres and a two-and-a-half-story, Italianate house in the rolling hills of Pittsburgh's fashionable East End, now Point Breeze. The home had been built for Benjamin and Caroline Vandervort between 1866 and 1872.

The Fricks spent twice that amount when they commissioned architect Andrew Peebles and renovated the interior of their new home.

According to records in the Frick Foundation Archives, Mr. Frick took personal interest in the remodeling and decorating of the eleven-room home, despite the growing demands of his industrial enterprises.

The Fricks took up residence at Clayton on January 29, 1883, and six weeks later, their first child, Childs, was born. Their son was followed by two daughters, Martha Howard in 1885, who died at the age of five, and Helen Clay in 1888. The Fricks' last child, Henry Clay Frick Jr., died a month after his birth in July 1892.

Clayton's second remodeling came in 1891, when the Fricks commissioned Frederick J. Osterling, a young Pittsburgh architect who expanded the house into a twenty-three room, four-story mansion, and A. Kimbel and Sons of New York, the primary decorators in the transformation.

Though the house on "Millionaire's Row" was an impressive one, the Fricks adorned their home with relative conservativism, choosing to refurbish instead of replace existing furnishings. The main reason for expansion was to accommodate the growing family.

In 1897, the Fricks once again felt the need for more space, and the Pittsburgh firm, Longfellow, Alden, and Harlow was hired to direct construction of the Greenhouse and Playhouse.

Clayton was redecorated a third time in 1901 by

Cottier and Company of New York which brought the mansion up to date with style that dismissed ornate Victorian business.

Around this time Frick's business activities shifted away from Pittsburgh to New York, and the family soon moved to 1 East 70th Street, New York City, now the location of The Frick Collection.

Helen Clay Frick remained passionately attached to Clayton, however, and against her father's wishes, held her coming-out party there instead of in New York, in December, 1908.

After the death of her parents, Henry in 1919, and Adelaide in 1931, Helen continued to visit and fund the upkeep of Clayton.

In May, 1981, Helen Clay Frick returned to her beloved Clayton where she died three years later on November 9 at the age of 96.

Miss Frick's devotion to her childhood home is responsible for the restoration of the estate which was opened to the public on September 22, 1990.

In her will, Frick decreed that Clayton should be maintained as intact as possible "for the purpose of public exhibition and preservation, as an historic house and estate..."

In response to her request that no alterations or additions be made which would in any way alter the estate's architectural style or the home's internal structure, a team of architects, historians, conservators and craftsman set to work restoring Clayton as it existed between 1882 and 1905, the years during which the home was inhabited by the Frick family.

Today, Clayton is an exceptional example of life in the late Victorian era. The house-museum is filled with original and recreated materials and personal mementos.

The Frick Art & Historical Center is a six-acre complex that includes not only Clayton, but the Frick Art Museum, featuring Helen Clay Frick's collection of European

10

paintings and decorative objects and traveling exhibitions from around the world; the Carriage museum, which houses a variety of carriages, sleighs, and automobiles owned by the Fricks; the rebuilt Greenhouse; the Museum Shop; and the Playhouse, now the Visitor's Center.

As one walks through the halls of Clayton, it's easy to envision the assemblage of international powers the home once entertained. President Theodore Roosevelt, First Lady Ida McKinley, Philander Knox, Andrew W. and Richard B. Mellon would be included in the historical review.

All that is missing from Clayton are the Fricks themselves, enjoying their home and what memoirs point to as an extremely important part of their life: Family.

In a 1990 Pittsburgh Press article, Patricia Lowry wrote, "From the clothing hanging on the hall rack to the brushes and combs on the bedroom bureaus, it looks as if Henry and Adelaide Frick have just stepped out and soon will return with their children...it isn't difficult to imagine all of that, to believe that just around the corner, just upstairs, just outside, the Fricks are still carrying on their privileged life."

Perhaps they are.

Charlie Stevens, Head of Security of the Frick Art & Historical Center at the time of writing, said he's heard and seen some strange things at Clayton.

"There are probably explanations," said Charlie. "I imagine in any old building you're going to hear things."

Nevertheless, Charlie concedes that the energy the mansion generates may still have a bit of Frick left in it.

The affable Mr. Stevens, who has been a guard at the mansion since 1986, says he's heard someone walking on the third floor steps at night when he was alone in the building.

And, in Mrs. Frick's bedroom, the room which Thierry Despont, a New York-based restorator whose credits include the Statue of Liberty, described as having "something magical" (about it), Stevens has seen depressions in the bed.

Charlie recalls that while on duty in Clayton his first

11

lap through the house, which included careful inspection of each room, would reveal nothing out of the ordinary.

On a later loop, he would occasionally see a depression on Mrs. Frick's bed in the room adorned with portraits of the family, and touched by the macabre with a death photo of little Henry.

Charlie speculates the specter may indeed be Mrs. Frick, returning to claim her position as matron of the mansion.

"Maybe because she was subdued in life, since Mr. Frick was the big man in the family, she's coming back for some glory now that she has her chance," he said.

Stevens also relayed tales of strange goings-on in the Frick Art Museum, during restoration of the house around 1989.

"They moved everything out of the house for renovations," he said. "A signal guard in the galleries had the doors close and lock behind him when no one else was around...and those doors never close. We think maybe Mrs. Frick was there. She went where her things went!"

Could it be that Mr. Frick's 1914 Rolls Royce Silver Ghost on display in the Carriage Museum is not the only ghost at The Frick estate?

Could it be that energy remains from the charged years of Frick inhabitation?

A pamphlet detailing the attractions of the Frick Art & Historical Center discusses some of the unexpectedly modest rooms in Clayton. "But be prepared for some surprises..." the brochure cautions.

Could it be architecture is not the only surprise in store?

Perhaps Mrs. Frick is part of the package.

•

A LIBRARY LOVE STORY

A relatively modern building that stands across the street from a bustling shopping center is the unlikely home to a classic romance. It is a ghost story, and it is a love story, and though it doesn't reside on the shelves or carry a Dewey Decimal number, the Dormont Public Library is proud to have this tale as part of its collection and its history.

Dee Krugh, an accomplished storyteller and mother of two, started work at the Dormont Library as a volunteer, and then went on to full time employment as a librarian at Dormont for six years.

Dee was willing to share the library's legend which she has taken time to refine into an intriguing tale fit for telling.

In her articulate and captivating fashion, she relayed the details.

"Mary, a librarian at Dormont, was a 'super-neat' person," Dee began. "Her love was the books, the library, and her husband, Joe.

"Everybody knew Mary. Kids came to her when they did papers because they knew Mary went the extra yard to help them out. She was a very attractive woman, very striking in appearance, and was very friendly."

And, according to Dee, she was very much in love with Joe and he with her.

Mardi Centinaro, a librarian currently working at Dormont, said, "She was just the kind of individual who loved the whole library environment. When her husband retired from his position as manager of the Dormont

Recreation Department, he couldn't drag her away from here. He wanted to travel, she wanted to work."

Centinaro characterized the popular librarian as firm, fair and friendly. Its no wonder the librarians speak so fondly of Mary.

"She was at the library one day and became very ill," said Dee. "They wanted to call the paramedics, but she wanted her Joe. They took her to St. Clair Hospital in Mt. Lebanon. She had a heart attack, remained in the hospital for a while, then went home to recuperate. All she looked forward to was getting back to the library.

"After she was healthy she was able to come back and worked for another year or a little less until she died one night in her sleep. This was in about 1987, and I would guess she was probably in her late 50s.

"The day she died we were having a program in the library, and Mary had ordered all the daffodils for the tables."

Dee commented on the ironic symbolism of the situation: The daffodils as Easter time icons, reflecting themes of death and rebirth. And, the date of Mary's death, tax day, April 15. Mary was the library's tax form guru, assisting patrons with their governmental duty.

"After she died, unusual things started to happen at the library," said Dee. "The Rolodex would start to spin, and no one would be there. We'd say, 'Mary, stop that!', and it would stop.

"You could really feel the energy in the place–it was Mary. Her husband used to come to the library just to sit there and feel her.

"You'd stand at the front desk working, and you'd swear she was standing behind you...but of course she wasn't," Dee said.

It seemed neither Joe nor death could take Mary from her beloved library. Could it be she continued work at Dormont even after her passing?

"You'd refer to a book you couldn't find, and all of a

sudden it would shoot out the shelf," said Dee.

"One time my niece needed some information for a report on the Olympics, and she said, 'Aunt Dee, do you think we could stop by the library?' It was closed at the time, but I had keys, so we went in. She told me what she wanted, and when we got there, the drawer of the card catalog was open to the exact item she wanted."

The strange activities in the library were not confined to ghostly reference assistance.

Mardi Centinaro said she witnessed a book not merely slide or drop but fly off the shelf of the mystery section.

She also said the lights often flickered in the building, but acknowledged that the malfunction was easily attributable to faulty wiring.

But there is more.

"We'd be in the back office where she often was, and you'd say something and it would happen," Dee reported. "One lady was moaning and groaning about her kid's hamster...she said she wished it was dead. That day, she went home and it was."

Other librarians corroborate the accounts of eerie coincidences which generated from workroom discussions.

Arlene Motus, a desk librarian who has worked nine years at Dormont said she witnessed similar situations. "When you were in the workroom, all you'd have to do is talk about something and it would happen," she said. "But of course it could be coincidental."

"I am a Christian person," said Arlene. "When I started working there, I thought there were some books on the shelves that shouldn't be there—things in the children's section about devils and such. I asked the head librarian about it, but she stood by the freedom of speech philosophy.

"There was one particular book that I used to place behind the other books—right where it should be—but behind the others. But somehow, that book was always back up front

15

with the others in the morning.

"We had volunteers who would check the shelves for order, but not enough that they would continually replace the book every day. I don't know how it got back into place all the time."

Perhaps Mary felt it her duty.

"Mary was buried at the Queen of Heavens Cemetery, out Route 19, in Upper St. Clair," said Dee. "Joe used to go to the cemetery a lot, and 10 months after Mary died the police found him dead in her car at the cemetery. Joe wasn't sick, but there he was, dead at the cemetery."

Mardi speculates that the lovelorn widower died of a broken heart. "I've heard they had some strange goings-on at the pool where he worked, too," she said. "It's like they didn't want to leave town."

If Mary wouldn't leave the library, did Joe compromise and follow her there?

"I used to work nights all the time," said Arlene. "My daughter and husband came to pick me up one night, and my daughter was in the vestibule waiting for me. I turned off all the lights and was walking by the copier machine when I heard a voice say, 'Hi'.

"I screamed and ran, and my daughter flew out the door. I said to my husband, 'Someone just said 'Hi' to me! He thought there was someone in the library, but I told him, 'No, the voice I heard was right by my ear, and there was nothing there but the wall'."

Mr. Motus searched the library but found no one, leaving Arlene to wonder if the voice she heard was that of John.

"He was a real nice person and was just so heartbroken when she died," she said. "He didn't want to live without her."

Shortly after Arlene received the ghostly greeting, the bizarre happenings slowed to a halt.

If Mary, and later Joe, were spectral inhabitants of the

16

Dormont Library, they have apparently moved on, perhaps to another plane.

"It was Mary's place to be and to stay–she just loved it," said Dee. "But the Rolodexes don't spin anymore.

"We think Mary waited there for Joe, and he came and got her and they're just not there anymore."

Separated by death.

Reunited by death.

Bound by love.

•

A VILLAINOUS GHOUL IN NORTH VERSAILLES

Shadowy figures showing human form, compact and swirling balls of light, and even life-like apparitions: All common manifestations of members of the spirit world.

But what about other displays of ghostliness?

A 52-year-old North Versailles woman claims she's had a brush with an unusual and terrifying type of specter. For Janet, the encounter which occurred 25 years ago is still a vivid memory.

"I raised my children by myself with all the usual fears a single parent has," she said. "My daughter was 13 and my son was eight when this happened."

Janet took a deep breath before she plunged into the story which she said still gives her chills.

"You're going to think I'm crazy, but I used to see a little person by the end of my bed," said Janet.

"I can describe him to a 'T'. He reminded me of a troll—human-like, but kind of 'trollish'. He had long brown hair, and had an elfin look about him. He was even shorter than a midget...he was so tiny...about a foot and a half tall.

"He never said anything—he just sat there, on the very end of the bed with his little legs draped over the side of the bed."

Having realized her story seems perhaps more difficult to believe than the 'garden variety' haunting of footsteps, voices, and strange occurrences, Janet paused to rationalize her experience.

18

"If you believe in God, you have to believe in the devil, too. I'm Catholic, and I know some of this contradicts our faith, but I know what I saw!

"At the time, I was working with a lady who was really into paranormal things. One day I told her about this, and she told me that there are demons that try to harm people. We talked about it quite extensively, and she gave me a prayer to say every night. I was afraid he was trying to harm my children."

Janet is sure her brushes with the man were not a product of a weary mind or a bright imagination. "I was not sleeping during any of this," she said. "The man was very clear, not foggy or as if he was at a distance. I could even pick out facial flaws on him.

"He appeared late at night, or early in the morning. I'd be asleep, I'd feel like there was a presence in the room, and I'd wake up and see him. I know I was awake.

"I'd ask him what he wanted, what he was doing there...then he would just go away. I just got so scared that I don't know exactly how he'd vanish, but he would.

"All of this happened six or seven times over the period of a few months. It was the most terrifying experience!

"But, eventually, he stopped coming. Maybe it was the prayer."

Janet reflects on the experience with a sense of puzzlement and relief.

"I don't know why he was there. Maybe there are things that sense your fears. I've heard the devil can read negative energy ...

"I never told my children about it, because I didn't want to scare them. They probably wouldn't believe it anyway."

●

THE DEAD MAN'S HELLO

"I was born in February of a leap year, so my birthday is kind of a strange date. And I've heard that people born in February are supposed to have an extra sense–I don't know if it's true or not–but sometimes I feel like I do."

These are the words of Jo from Plum, who says her husband thinks she is the victim of an overactive imagination.

Nevertheless, Jo seems to be susceptible to signals from the spirit world, and often utilizes extra sensory faculties. Even her disbelieving husband acknowledges her uncanny sensibilities.

"Sometimes I tell him what he's going to do or say," she said. "I've told him what he's hungry for, I've told him what he's going to say next...things like that. Maybe it's because I believe in it, I don't know."

Jo's experiences are not limited to what some might term coincidence. She's sure she's had at least one apparitional pass with the paranormal.

"We used to go to Kings Restaurant and Lounge in Monroeville, a place that is no longer in business," she said. "There was a young man, Dave, who was a cook there. He wasn't really a hippy type, but he was into drugs and drinking and that. He was extremely quiet, but he used to stand at the end of the bar and he'd say hello and things like that.

"I went to college for restaurants and management, and since he was a cook, we used to talk about things like that a lot.

"One evening my husband and I went into the lounge and sat down at the end of their very long bar. I looked over, and there was Dave, walking down past me. I said, 'Hi', and he said, 'hi'.

"So, my husband and I sat there for a while and talked to the waitress, and eventually, the conversation came around to Dave.

"She said, 'Didn't you hear about him?'

"I said, 'No, what?'

"She said he died of an overdose of drugs that night before.

"I told her not to kid about things like that, and that I had just said hello to him.

"Well, we went on like that for a little while, and soon I was convinced that she was serious and he really had died. But I swore I saw him walk down behind us at the bar. It was him, no one else.

"He looked plain as day, just like he always did."

As she told her story, Jo questioned the whys behind the strange experience.

"Why does that happen? Why do spirits linger? I don't know why other people can't see this! We had just walked in, it's not as if we were drinking or anything.

"Could it be because we had some kind of a strange past life bond or something? Was there some strange connection and that's why I could see him?"

We'll never know, Jo.

•

THE STINGY SPOOK OF BEECHVIEW

Mere mention of the words "secret room" conjures thoughts of intrigue, mystery, and perhaps a tinge of the supernatural.

Imagine an untouched region of a home, an unexplored crawl space the length of a standard parlor.

Imagine this dark and secluded section in the bowels of the building that for whatever reason never realized its original intent of human occupation.

Or did the builder have alternative plans for this space? And why was the compartment never completed?

These are some of the questions that Michelle, a Carnegie Mellon University student, asks about her home in Beechview.

Michelle presented her tale in a careful manner, certain to lay an historical foundation before plunging into the more ethereal aspects of her story.

"My house was built in the 1920's by a man who owned a candy store and supposedly had a lot of money," she said. "Everyone says that he didn't believe in banks, so he hid all of his money in the house. Neighbors have told me that he used to scream out his windows, 'Stay away from my money!'"

Most of Michelle's information about the original owner of her home has come from neighbors.

"They told me his first wife died and he remarried, and when he eventually passed away, his second wife ended

22

up going a little bit wacky. Nobody saw her for a while, so they got the health department to go down to the house and check on her to make sure she was O.K.

"When they found her, she was just really losing it. She went kind of insane, and didn't change for months and smelled really bad.

"There was a little nickel and dime store on the corner of the block, and before they took her away, they say that one day she went into the store to buy something and pulled out a hundred dollar bill. The woman behind the counter said, 'Where did you get that money?'

"She said that she had found it under the rug in her house. So, it just became known that he hid his money in the house, and that there was still money laying around after he died.

"Still, no one knows if the money is still in the house–if he hid it somewhere. Maybe the health department took it when they came to take her away. Maybe the two families that have lived there since he did got it...no one knows."

Except for, perhaps, the hoarder himself.

"When my Dad bought the house he went looking for the money, but didn't find anything. But there was one place he didn't check.

"We have an unexcavated room in our basement, and he never checked there. If the room was dug a little bit more, it could be a full room, but it was never finished. For some reason, my Dad just never checked there. He was planning on it, but never got to it."

The home offered more than the titillation of the prospects of an in-house fortune, however. For Michelle and her family, this was only the beginning.

"When I was about a year old, in 1975, there were two incidents where an old man came to the house.

"My mother told me she was in the kitchen one night and looked out the screen door, and this man was standing

23

there. She said, 'Can I help you?' He didn't say anything, so she asked him again. After a long pause he said, "Yes, I think you can.'

"She asked him what he needed or what she could do, and he didn't say anything, so finally she told him, 'I think you had better go,' and he left.

"About a week later she was coming home one evening, and started walking up the steep hill to our front door. There are two flights of steps, and when she was on the first landing, she saw a silhouette of that man at the top of the stairs. She said again, 'Sir, can I help you?'

"He said, 'Yes, I think you can.' She asked him what he wanted, and when he didn't answer, she said, 'Please leave, this is my house!' And he left, and that was the end of that for a while, until a couple of years ago, when my brother, who is now 15, saw an old man on the porch. But I don't remember any of the details."

Michelle and her mother naturally wonder if the strange old man could have been an apparition of the original owner, come to claim his cache, or perhaps to keep tabs on the new family in his home.

Not necessarily the stuff of great hauntings, but the story's supernatural status intensifies.

"Right after I was born, my Mom was lying on the couch watching TV, and I was in a baby swing near our fireplace. She told me she glanced over at me, and there was a little child standing next to me. She said she blinked and looked back, and it was gone.

"I wonder what that means since it was standing next to *me*," she said, sounding a little spooked.

This is not the only time unfamiliar children have been seen in the home. Michelle's father, whom she characterizes as "extremely skeptical", said he is certain he saw a little girl in pigtails standing by his bed one morning when he awoke.

"There's been small stuff like that," Michelle said.

"Small stuff," like the many times her mother feels

as if someone is trying to pull her out of bed.

"There was also a time recently when my Mom had her sister visiting from Florida. They heard chains scraping up the side of the house and across the roof and down the other side of the house.

"I wasn't home at the time, and they called me and told me what happened. She also called the police, because they were terrified and didn't know what to do. The police didn't find anything."

Despite her fear, the inviting prospect of discovering money finally drew Michelle and a friend to the basement in 1993.

"We wanted to go in there with a video camera and dig up some of the bricks and dirt to see if we could find anything," she said.

"We thought we were going to find money—we thought, 'This is great! We're going to be rich!'"

The girls got more than they'd bargained for.

"There's no light down there, no windows because it's all underground. We had masks on, because it seemed like there was a lot of dirt down there. We brought the video camera, flashlights, and a lamp with an extension cord.

"We went in there, and found toys! There was a coloring book...we tried to look for a date but couldn't find one. The book was really destroyed from being underground, but we could tell that some of the pages were colored in.

"We also found a baseball bat, and wheels to a truck that looked like they were old. And, we found some Christmas balls. My Mom said she didn't recognize any of the items, and didn't think the toys belonged to any of us.

"We were going to put the toys back into the room because we were afraid that if there were spirits, that they'd get ticked off if we took their toys! But my Mom's fiance accidentally threw them away because we had them in a bag, and since they were dirty they looked like garbage."

The basement held even more surprises.

"There ended up being another unexcavated room with a pile of dirt in it next to the first one," said Michelle. "We wanted to go in there, too, but the flashlight we had was dim and it was just so dark.

"As the night went on the battery just kept dying and dying and dying...and at one point, all the lights went dead."

It's not difficult to imagine the tension of the moment. Michelle continued in a tone growing ever anxious.

"The flashlight, the lamp, and even the video recorder–they all just died. We got really scared and freaked out and thought maybe it was a sign, so we got out of there as fast as we could. I was the last one out, and it was an awful feeling trying to crawl through that little space in pitch black wondering what was behind you.

"We tried to put everything together and thought maybe the man who built the house was trying to give us a sign to get out if there was money in there. And maybe the toys belonged to the little girl my Dad saw, and maybe that's who my Mom saw standing by me.

"The whole thing scared us, and we finished the video saying we weren't going back in the room."

Mom had a different idea. Her desire for additional storage space was far stronger than any fear of the unknown.

"She went in there one day to start to clean the room up, and all of a sudden she screamed for me to come down there," Michelle said. "She had found bones."

Those bones now reside in Michelle's dorm room, testament to her fascination with the morbid and mysterious.

"The biggest bone looked like a joint and it still had a little bit of cartilage on it," she said. "There were even calcium deposits. There were a lot of smaller pieces of bone, too.

"I took it to a professor who immediately knew it was lamb bone. I don't know why they'd bury a lamb down there ..."

Could the strange findings be explained by the

possibility that previous occupants of the home used the unexcavated room as a compost pile or garbage heap?

Michelle doesn't think so. If this were the case, shouldn't she, and later her mother, have found more refuse than they did?

Regardless, she is convinced there is something strange about her home.

"I really feel there's something there—a spirit—in my house. But as far as it being evil, I don't get any bad vibes from it. Nobody's gotten hurt, and it's nothing threatening.

"Sometimes I feel content, other times I feel scared. For some reason when I was really little I always wanted my room to be in the attic. I didn't get it until I was 14 or 15 when my parents turned it into my bedroom.

"I always went up there and looked out and it just felt so good to be up there. It still does—I feel safest in the attic. When I'm down on the first floor, though, I often get the chills. I keep thinking I'm going to look out on the porch and see the old man.

"I feel like I lose things all the time in my house. Sometimes I get mad and I'll just start talking to them: 'Ha ha, really funny...I've had enough already!' I feel more comfortable when I do that, because I feel that if they are there, they know that I know.

"There's a lot of people who are afraid of my house for one reason or another," Michelle said.

With its reputation, it's no wonder.

•

THE GHOSTLY GROWL

Many a hound has woofed and snuggled his way into the hearts of his family, institutionalizing himself as a true member of the clan.

Be the bowser a mongrel or purebred, he is a respected and cherished inhabitant of the home, and to lose him would be a great emotional blow for the household.

Such was the case for members of a Dormont family, who believe their pooch may be lingering, in a paranormal kind of way.

Tiger passed away in the summer of 1992, and since then, Annette, a respected member of the Dormont community, has heard him about the house.

"We had Tiger for 10 years," she said. "A few months after he died I heard him growl.

"He had this thing with trying to wake you up in the middle of the night so you would take him out, and there was this noise he'd make when he was doing that.

"One night I was watching TV really late, and I heard that noise–I definitely wasn't asleep!

"Other times I heard a car door slam here, and I'd hear him growl, like he used to at noises like that.

"My husband thinks I'm crazy...but he's heard it, too," she said.

"My dog died in our bedroom–he died a terrible death. There was something wrong with his back. We took him to two different vets, he got worse, then he got better.

"We brought him home, but he must have caught something at the vet's because he got really bad and died right

28

here on the bed. I don't know if that has anything to do with what's going on with the dog voices right now..."

The canine commotion may be fairly light-weight haunting material, easily explained with the supposition that fond memories of fido are encroaching on real life.

But there is more to add to this 65-year-old home's supernatural docket.

"I see things continuously that go right past me," said Annette. "It isn't exactly a figure, but more of a shadow."

Apparently Tiger saw the figure as well.

"When Tiger was alive, about twice he acted very strange. He looked up in the air, back and forth and back and forth, at nothing, then he cried and ran behind the sofa in the living room.

"About 6 months after that, my husband was alone with the dog and he did it again. And he was not a scaredy-cat dog."

Annette continued to rattle off the list of strange occurrences her family has experienced in the home.

"Our TVs and VCRs go on and off, but there probably could be some reason for that.

"But I get odd feelings all the time. I guess it's a premonition type of thing, but lately I know what my daughter's going to say...I know exactly what she's going to tell me.

"She had an accident on October 31st of this year, and I knew it. Now, when the phone rings, I tell whoever is around at the time who is calling and what they want, ahead of time–before I answer the phone–so they don't think I'm being silly."

If there are unearthly guests in Annette's home, they seem to have developed a fondness for her.

"About two months ago, I was leaning over the bathtub with my head under the faucet washing my hair. I felt my something touching my arm, and I figured it was a shampoo bottle. But when I looked, there was nothing there.

"And I've felt a warm hand brushing the hair off my forehead! I'm scared of a lot of things, but for some reason, that didn't scare me."

Annette's oldest daughter, Connie, has also experienced the presence.

"One night Connie was in her room, on her bed with the lights on," Annette said. "She heard a noise, scratching back and forth on the floor.

"She looked down and the end of her stereo plug was moving back and forth–all by itself–on the floor. It wasn't plugged in, and there was nothing near it. From then on, she's slept with the lights on."

Annette relayed more of Connie's strange encounters.

"One day she was running up the stairs, and as she turned to go up our landing, something swooshed past her–a flashing figure of light. She was really frightened, and flew down the steps to us."

Annette believes most of the supernatural activity in the house centers in the upstairs hallway. Apparently, that's the place to spot a spook in this Dormont home.

"Connie has seen a lot more than I have," said Annette. "Recently she said, 'Mom, you're not going to believe this, but I'm start to see things ... I'm seeing parts of a body–I saw a leg.'

"I said, 'Oh, come on!' But one day, I told the girls I work with about this. Our secretary's sister was married to a guy who lived in our house, and here she got really white.

"Apparently, the woman who had lived there at one time had her legs amputated.

"I never knew about the woman, and I never told my daughter."

Despite the spectral evidence that points to the possibility that Annette may indeed inhabit a haunted house, she's still not entirely convinced she shares her home with a spook, or even a 'presence', let alone an apparitional amputee.

"It's just something we've lived with," she said. "It's

not damaging or anything."

"When Shelly sees things now it has more of a shape.
I think if I'd hear hear something or start seeing something
more ...

"I don't know, you can usually tell if something's
harmful or not. I say, as long as it doesn't appear..."

•

A GHOST IN THE FLOWER SHOP

One of the Pittsburgh area's oldest flower shops is located in the tiny, hardscrabble town of Etna.

Michael Blaha Flowers has endured a lot in its more than 90 years of existence.

"This town was really happening when the mills were here," said David Kornely, current owner of the shop.

But a lot has changed since Mr. Blaha and his flower cart strolled the streets of Etna around the turn of the century.

"Full Service Florist Since 1900" boasts the shop's card and answering machine.

What isn't blazened on the business card, however, is that the place has a ghost at least that old. Kornely says the spirit of an eight-year-old boy named Peter has resided in the Bridge Street building for about 100 years.

"Because I'm from Etna, I had heard the stories about the building being haunted before I even bought the place," said Kornely. "I never believed any of it, and ghosts don't bother me anyway!"

Now he believes it.

Kornely sat with us on a rainy, quiet afternoon in the elegant shop which, complete with a couch and coffee table, resembles more of a home than a business. It's easy to see why Peter would find this a comfortable resting place.

"Prior to when I bought Blaha's, I had looked at this building and thought I might open up a shop of my own in this place," he said. "But I never spoke to the landlord about it, because after thinking about it, I figured it was kind of stupid to open a flower shop against Michael Blaha's (on

Butler Street), which is so established. So what I did, was I bought Blaha's and moved it down here!"

"When I wanted to move my shop down here, the landlord said, 'I'm not going to lie to you, the place is haunted.'"

The exact history of the building is unknown to Kornely and the current landlord and owner, Kevin Burke. However, the men have ascertained that the building was once the Colonial House Hotel, or the Colonial Inn, and later a tavern and a restaurant. Kornely said the building was also once a bordello.

"Apparently Peter was an illegitimate child who lived in this building in a third floor apartment with his mother, who was one of the women in the bordello.

"I've heard that he wasn't allowed out much and somehow or another he got a hold of firecrackers and a fire was started, and he was killed in the fire."

Kevin Burke said he found evidence supporting reports of a fire. As he was remodeling the second and third floors into apartments, he discovered burn marks on the walls.

And an incident involving one of Burke's tenants points to a possible fear of fire on Peter's part.

According to *The Herald*, a local newspaper, Burke said:

"I had a tenant on the third floor who used a kerosene heater. He kept the kerosene on the second floor, which I thought was a very good safety measure. One day I found the pump from the can in a sink on the second floor and the can of kerosene in the basement. When the tenant saw me he said to me, 'I see you don't like the way I have been keeping my kerosene.'

"'I said, 'I don't know what you mean.'

"'Well,' he said, 'I see it's been moved to the basement. I didn't do it.'

'Neither did I,' I said. And nobody lives on the

second floor."

This prank typifies Peter's behavior in the building. Never malicious but always mischievous, he likes to rearrange and play with things and occasionally even initiates physical contact with the humans in his domicile.

Many tenants in the building have been "touched" by Peter.

"Apparently when Kevin was restoring the building, Peter caused an awful lot of trouble for these two women who had a shop in here at one time," said Kornely.

"I heard they had a seance in here, and they really upset him!"

Sharpsburg sisters Nancy and Audrey Vecchio ran "Echoes", a gift and antique shop, from 1977 to 1982 on the first floor of the building where the flower shop is now located.

"People would tell me that they would come in in the morning and everything from their desk would be thrown on the floor, their pencils would be broken, and antique dolls would be thrown all around," Kornely said.

"People would be in the store and have their hair pulled, rocking chairs would move, and for no known reason, the place would get cold."

The Herald reported the Vecchios also witnessed teacups turning over and doors suddenly opening or closing by themselves. Keys could be heard jingling, and the sudden odor of paint would saturate the room when no one and no paint was in sight.

Audrey Vecchio told *The Herald*: "I once had an actual levitation. I remember I was doing a table arrangement and was holding a candle when suddenly, across the table from me another candle began to rise in the air...and I couldn't see anyone holding that candle."

In another article about the shop, the Vecchio's colleague, Pat Bollinger, was reported to have heard someone call her name.

The sisters told the newspaper they believed Peter slept in a crib they used to display dolls. The Vecchios would come into the shop to find the dolls in the crib lying in a disorderly fashion, and a quilt which was usually folded on the crib rail was found on the floor.

Items in the store were continually misplaced by unseen forces. Toys were moved, candles continually overturned, pages torn out of a workbook, and a heavy hook which hung in the wall was found on the floor, seven feet across the room.

According to the newspaper article, the sisters witnessed, in the absence of breeze, the violent shaking of a tree hung with little animals.

Heavy footsteps in the front room when the sisters went to the back room indicated what they felt to be discontentment on Peter's part. The Vecchios hypothesized he didn't like to be left alone.

The naming of the spirit came late in his stay in the building. *The Herald* reported that a psychic told the Vecchios he could sense the presence in the building of a slightly built, poor, dark-haired eight-year-old boy named Peter.

Kevin Burke had previously named the wraith Ralph. But with the psychic's declaration, the playful entity was henceforth known as Peter.

This was not the only time a psychic came to the building. The flower shop and its haunted history were the subjects of a Halloween radio show featuring a psychic.

"She was from Gary and Beth's morning show on 92.9," said Kornely. "She was here for about nine hours to tape the entire show.

"She was in the basement and felt his presence. Apparently she was in contact with him, and he liked what I'd done to the shop and felt comfortable here, and apparently that's why he's never really done anything destructive to the place."

But Peter certainly has caused a lot of devilish disorder about the shop for Kornely and his customers.

"When I first moved down here, before I officially opened up, I spent some here by myself and with the landlord as he was putting on the finishing touches and restoring a lot of things," he said.

"A month prior to me opening the business in this building I put a big paper sign in the window announcing Michael Blaha was coming to this location soon.

"This sign was really secured–I mean it was really up there, and there was no way it was going to come down. It was very straight, very nice and neat.

"I came in the next day, and the sign was on the window, but it was like a little kid would have put it up–wrinkled, and all funny. There was no way that sign could have done that by itself."

In addition to his fascination with toys, candles, and apparently signs, Peter seemed to, as Kornely said, "like mechanical things."

"I had a new answering machine that worked fine–there was no problem with it. But when I came down here I could not get that machine to work for anything. I even had the telephone company come back three and four times. They spent hours here, but it would not work.

"So, I just gave up on it, shut it off, and over a period of two months–March and April–stuff just eventually piled up on top of it.

"We have three lines here, and it's a rollover. So in other words, if the first number is busy it just rolls over to the second and then the third line.

"Well, Mother's Day weekend, two lines were busy and the third line started to ring and there was nobody to answer it.

"All of a sudden, the answering machine came on and began to work by itself. It had never worked! The phone company couldn't get it to work, we couldn't get it to work.

"Periodically, it worked for a long time, then every once in a while it would just go goofy–it wouldn't work. The only thing that we can figure is that it was one of his play toys ... he liked it."

The cash register was Peter's next "play toy." "We'd come in in the morning and the thing would be totally unprogrammed."

Peter seemed to develop an interest in gardening as well.

"That same Mother's Day weekend I had special dish gardens made up, and in the dish gardens were violets, and there were violets and tulips in the backs of the gardens.

"I was the last to leave at night and the first to come in in the morning. No one else was in there overnight. I came in in the morning, and there was dirt all over that tile floor, and the tulips were replanted in the dish garden in a different place, and the dish garden itself was in a different place."

Kornely said the plant, which he has dubbed, "Peter's dish garden" blooms constantly, perhaps tended by a ghostly green thumb.

"We had stuffed animals disappear, too," said Kornely. "We had two sets of dogs–a mother and a puppy. We sold both puppies and one mother, but the other mother was still here.

"One day I came in and the dog was gone. I asked one of the people who works here, 'Did you sell the dog?'

"She said, 'No, I thought you did.'

"We looked and looked for that dog, but we couldn't find it anywhere. About eight months later we were upstairs and we found it inside the plastic bag with all the extra stuffed animals. No one had put it in there!"

Hair pulling seems to be another one of Peter's favorite pranks.

"There was a girl who worked here who had long blond hair," said Kornely. "One day I heard this scream from downstairs, and I ran down into the basement and said,

'What happened?!'

"She said that he had pulled her hair!"

The Vecchios experienced a similar incident. They told *The Herald* that a customer's son once sat and began to rock in a rocking chair in the shop when suddenly he shouted that someone was pulling his hair. Apparently Peter didn't want to share the rocker!

Nancy Vecchio also reported she felt someone playing with her hair as she sat embroidering in the shop.

Peter's acitivities were not confined to the first floor and basement of the building.

"He would navigate all around the building," said Kornely. "He'd be in here in the shop for a while, then he'd go back up to his original apartment.

"The woman who just moved from there–she's very reliable–she is a manager at WQED. She'd be sound asleep and all of a sudden her bed would just start rocking like mad and she'd get up and say, 'Peter, stop it,' and it would stop."

Burke has experienced 'Peter' on the other floors of the building as well. While he was using an electric drill, Peter unplugged three sections of extension cord and locked the door of the room to the electrical outlet, reported *The Herald.*

"When Kevin actually moved into his apartment on the third floor (because that's the first one he finished remodeling), his television would come on all the time," said Kornely. "He finally had to take the remote control and hide it.

"Kevin has workers who will not come into this building. One of them has actually seen Peter materialize in front of him..."

The young specter has even turned up in a photograph of the shop published in *The Herald*–or so sees Kornely. True, these writers were able to discern what appeared to be a face peaking from behind some greenery. But is it really a phantom image, or merely a distortion of light?

David Kornely is not afraid of the ghost which may wander through his flower shop, slightly disrupting business on an often daily basis. In fact, he seems to regard him with a certain affection.

"I used to come in all the time and say, 'Good morning, Peter' and 'Goodbye, Peter' and 'Take care of the shop, Peter.'

"But the strangest thing has happened. Peter has disappeared! Ever since last Halloween he has not been around...he is nowhere.

"It's funny, a girl who worked here has the answering machine now...and all of a sudden it's wacky, so I wonder if maybe he's *there*–I don't know!"

The Herald article posed the theory that a blessing of the building may have removed Peter from the premises. Kornely said an Etna businesswoman requested the ceremony, and he did not object.

Father Joseph Luisi, parochial vicar of All Saint's Church, Etna, performed the blessing which consisted of a reading from the Scriptures, prayers, and a sprinkling of holy water.

According to Kornely, the blessing was not unlike one conducted for newlyweds moving into a new home.

Nothing unusual occurred during the blessing, and Kornely said it had no effect on Peter's activity at the time.

Kornely seems a little disheartened at the thought that Peter may be gone for good.

A look inside Blaha's reveals nary a spook, but a fresh and tranquil atmosphere.

Stained glass windows and skylights provide vehicles through which warm sunbeams reflect to dance mysteriously on hardwood floors. High ceilings and verdant decor lend a rustic airiness to the tidy, cheerful shop. Kornely's artistic flair displays itself in every smartly-hung piece of art, every adornment, every bauble, and of course every plant and flower. Michael Blaha Flowers is far removed from the sterile, counter shop common to the trade.

"This is what a flower shop should be like," said Kornely.

And, every once in a while, something happens that rekindles Kornely's hope that the gentle ghost is still around.

As this book was going to press, a long-dormant Italian clock started ticking on its own once again.

The ghost?

Perhaps.

As with many other tales of the supernatural, there is never really an ending.

•

SARAH COMES HOME

Pittsburgh maintains hundreds of historical sites and one need not look far to find well-preserved remnants of the past. Old buildings–many more than 100 years old–are not a rarity in this city.

With a little investigation, it isn't difficult to find such a place as the Frick mansion–an ideal setting for a haunt–which does, in fact, have a ghost.

Suburbia, however, with its shopping malls and townhouse complexes, seems an unlikely spot for spook sighting.

But the spirit world knows no provincial boundaries, and extends beyond the city lines into Pittsburgh's environs and finally, into the countryside of Allegheny County.

The following story comes from an affluent area in Mt. Lebanon. The settlement Franklin Toker in his book, *Pittsburgh, An Urban Portrait,* called, "the archetype of the wealthy Pittsburgh suburb" may not seem prime for the haunting.

At least one family would disagree.

"My Aunt Sarah died on April 16, 1968," said Elizabeth, a freshman English major at Carnegie Mellon University.

"Soon afterwards, my grandparents bought a house in Mt. Lebanon. It was a totally square house that you would draw. They lived there for 18 years."

It was in this typical, modern home that the restless soul of a life cut short roamed for years, comforting her familial successors.

"Sarah died an unexpected, malpractice type of death," said Elizabeth. "She had been sick and somehow things escalated–all of a sudden she was being operated on for no reason, and she died."

The tragedy was naturally a blow to Sarah's family, which included five children. It seems the young mother felt a need to comfort her parents, however, and for many years made their home her own ghostly abode.

"Soon after Sarah died my grandparents would be in bed, and my grandmother would wake up and hear what sounded like people fighting in the attic," said Elizabeth.

"She said it sounded like people running around up there. She told me, 'The noise was terrific.'

"The first time they heard this my grandfather went upstairs and found nothing. Then, about a week after that they heard a huge crash one night along with the other noises they had heard before.

"The next day, my grandmother went up in the attic and found Sarah's huge, very heavy cedar chest face down on the floor. This was a really heavy piece–nothing would have knocked it over."

There was other evidence of Sarah's presence in the home.

"In her dining room, my grandmother had Sarah's wedding picture. One day she came home from being out somewhere and found it lying on the floor behind a chair. Now if it had fallen down, it wouldn't be there behind the chair."

Was this Sarah's way of signaling her mother–alerting her to her post mortem wishes?

"My grandmother wanted Sarah to be buried in the family plot in the cemetery, but for some reason, Sarah's husband wouldn't allow it and had her placed in a mausoleum.

"He died of cancer about four or five years ago, and my grandmother tried to have her moved to the family plot then, but the husband has to approve something like that.

"This is all really upsetting to my grandmother. She gets extremely upset–it's her daughter–and she feels like she never really got to rest because of the burial arrangements."

Could the disturbances be Sarah's way of asking her mother to help her to "rest?"

Sarah's parents found other signs of what they thought to be their daughter about the home.

"They had a big buffet with a glass top in the dining room," said Elizabeth. "Above it was a huge mahogany mirror. If the mirror were to fall off its hook it would fall straight down and crash the glass.

"Again, my grandparents came home one day to find the mirror propped up against the buffet. No one had been in their home, and there's no way the mirror would have been propped up like that had it fallen."

Elizabeth has witnessed one of entity's most common habits.

"For a while, during the summer when they kept the door open, it would slowly but methodically close at 11:00 p.m. almost every night," she said. "There was no breeze–nothing. Everyone just knew it was Sarah coming home.

"Though I never met her, I heard so much about her and felt like I almost knew her," she said. "I used to think it was really neat and wished I was there when more things happened!"

The supernatural events ceased about ten years after Sarah's death. The 'square house' now belongs to another family, and Elizabeth said her grandmother misses her daughter's presence.

"She was never frightened of anything that happened–she always thought that Sarah just wanted her to know that she was there."

•

THE PHANTOM
IN THE FIRE HOUSE

"In the late 1800's, the city of Allegheny grew rapidly, creating a need for an expanded fire department. Troy Hill's Fire Company #11, Truck Company E, was organized and assigned to duty at Branch and Forest Streets, today called Ley and Froman. When the city of Allegheny became part of the city of Pittsburgh on Dec. 6, 1907, all fire companies were renumbered, and ours on Troy Hill became #51."

These words are taken from a flyer which is distributed by the proud members of the Troy Hill Fire Company. It proclaims the company's history in a concise and thorough fashion.

"In the 1920's, the city began to mechanize the fire service. The last to use horses, our fire station received a chain-driven American LaFrance on January 16, 1927, and the Reo Service Ladder Truck on April 21, 1927.

"To clear up confusion about how many engine houses were actually in use, they were renumbered again, and Troy Hill's became Company #39"

From the early 1970's until 1988, "building deterioration and a lack of repair funds" threatened to close the station.

"...after a long, determined struggle, against all odds, the battle to keep our fire house was won by the whole community under the Leadership of Troy Hill Citizens Inc."

Many citizens and area firemen are familiar with the long-standing fight the company has waged against the city of

44

Pittsburgh to ensure the continued existence of Engine House #39. Recent studies from city consultants suggest downsizing the fire force may be the way to go.

Citizens may *not* be acquainted, however, with all company happenings, or with the *unpaid* firemen who seem to inhabit the house.

Two prominent Troy Hill residents, both instrumental in the fight for the fire house, were contacted during the course of research for this volume. Neither realized the hall is a haunted one.

At the time of writing, Donald Dorsey presides over Company #39. This exuberant chief clearly respects his station, and is quick to impart the company's history and its tales, one of which involves a ghost.

Or maybe two.

Or more.

In fact, one Troy Hill fireman said he saw a table-full of ghostly firemen in the basement of the building.

Chief Dorsey freely admits to a belief in the supernatural. City fireman John Arnold does not.

Both men have experienced the specters.

Neither can find cause to dismiss the unearthly occurrences in the fire station as coincidence or product of natural phenomena.

We wound our way up Troy Hill in search of the station's spirits, and found at least a chilling reenactment of one fireman's frightful nights in the building.

As we made our spiral ascent to the bunk room, a place the firemen call a center of supernatural activity, Don Dorsey began to unravel the building's story.

Until 1989, the house featured wooden floors, and today retains its spiral staircase and working pole, lending a charming touch of history to the well-maintained building.

"The bunk room was built for about twelve guys," he said. "There is a guy here, George–I've worked with him since 1980–and for the first time in 1985 he told me that someone would pull the blankets off him while he was sleeping up here. It wasn't any of the other guys doing it. He said the bed would shake, too.

"The first time a girl was assigned to our company, we were cautioned about sexual harassment. So, we didn't want to tell her someone might pull the covers off her!

"The first week she was here she came down one night and said, 'Thanks a lot! You guys didn't even tell me!' She had experienced it, too."

John Arnold had a different bunk room experience.

"The pole hole covering in the bunk room has been known to drop by itself," he said. "The lid that covers the sliding area around the pole is fairly heavy–there's no way it could lift up by itself. But, when we're up here sleeping, it has banged like someone lifted it up and then dropped it. It's a very distinct sound."

An ear-reaching grin consumed John's face as he dropped the cover for all to hear. The clamor echoed eerily in the spacious, sparsely furnished room.

"When you hear it and you were asleep, first you pull yourself off the floor, then you think, 'Who in the hell did that?!'" he said. "But no one ever did it–everyone else is asleep in their beds."

Don reported a number of other unexplained disturbances in the building.

"A lot of nights when there was only three men here, they'd all be downstairs and say, 'Who's up in the office? Who's doing the lights? Who's doing the drawers in the office up there?' And there was nobody here! You're often downstairs when no one is upstairs and hear the lockers open and footsteps and things like that..."

During the 1989 remodeling of the station, Dorsey said he would check the building compulsively to make sure the work was progressing as specified in the renovation plans.

"I was the only one besides the general contractor

who had the key, and I'd come in here every night to make sure they weren't ripping out the staircase or the pole or something," he said.

"Of course you always get creepy feelings in a big old empty building, but it's *my* empty building and I know it better than anybody.

"One night I walked in and there were paint cans everywhere all over the floor. I left to do something, but came back in an hour and they were all stacked in a pyramid–and there was nobody else here! Nobody else had a key, and the contractor didn't do it."

Our tiny troupe of fire fighters and ghost hunters moved through the building to the back bunk room, where John relayed his most striking supernatural experience.

The back bunk room is small in comparison to most of the rooms in the station. The room contains the steep wooden staircase leading to the roof of the building where the top of the hose tower is located.

"When I first came here back in 1988 we all slept up front in the main bunk room and this back room was just a locker room," said John.

"It's really noisy in the front bunk room–busses, kids, people coming out of the bar room at 2 o'clock in the morning–things like that. So, after being here a while I said, 'There's a big back room here and nothing going on, except for people going to the hose tower, why don't we put a bed or two back here?' They said, 'If that's what you want to do, go ahead.'

"So, I dragged a bed back there. It was just a big empty room with lockers. That was before we had the new windows, and the old ones rattled when the wind blew and that. But it was still fairly nice and quiet."

"Nobody ever said anything to me about a ghost or anything like that, so I know that this story I'm telling you is not psychosomatic. It's not as if guys said, 'Oh, you don't want to sleep in that back room!' or, 'Ooh, the devil is coming through here!' I didn't know anything. I was a new guy in off the street and they didn't tell me anything like that.

"I put my bed in the corner over there." John gesticulated to a bed nestled snuggly in the corner of the room. "Eventually, there were three of us sleeping back here, but I was in here by myself for a long time. Everyone said I was crazy because you can feel the temperature difference back here—it's cold—there's only one radiator."

John paused for a moment as if he was questioning his initial willingness to relate his experience.

"I'm the kind of guy who will eliminate everything before I even start to believe in any kind of ghost story," he began again.

"Don will tell you this too, because he's known me for a long time. If I hear a noise—if the door bangs or the locker bangs, I go over and investigate to find out what caused it...not that there's anything in there, but the wind blew it, or something like that."

Something like that.

"So I'm sleeping back here one night and everything's quiet, and you can hear everything—you're used to all the sounds—this is our house. You know if someone's walking across the floor. I know the difference between this bolt sliding on this door, and this bolt sliding over here on this door." John slid the creaky bolts, demonstrating the slight nuances in sound.

"I sleep with my head under the covers to keep warm because it's cold back here. I'm sleeping, and I'll show you exactly what I hear—I hear this: "

John quickly opened the door to the hose tower, moved onto the first step, closed the door behind him and quietly positioned himself halfway up the staircase, setting up his reenactment.

With measured, heavy steps, he clunked down the stairs, opened and purposefully banged the door against the wall it opens to, trudged across the room to a locker and clanged it open.

"I figured it was one of these guys–probably Don because he's always going up to the hose tower. So, I keep my head under the covers and don't pay any attention. Then I hear whoever was down at the locker walk back across the floor, and go back up the stairs.

"So now I'm getting a blast of cold air. I'm laying right here, and the cold air coming down from the tower just goes right on top of me. And I'm waiting for the guy who went up there to come back down and close the door. And I'm freezing here!"

Don inserts an explanatory note. "Nobody who goes up to the tower closes the door behind them–they wait to close it until they come back down," he said. "The worst thing would be for somebody to lock that door behind you, because then you'd be stuck up on the roof since the door locks from the inside–from the bunk room."

John continued. "Finally, I looked around and didn't see anyone, so I got up and locked the door. I went down the stairs and said to the guys, 'Next time you come up here and go to the hose tower, lock the damn door–I'm freezing up there!'

"They all said nobody was up there. I said, 'Don't tell me! I know what I heard!' They said I was sleeping–I was in la-la land. I said, 'No I wasn't!'

"So, to eliminate things a little more, I think: So the hose tower door was unlocked to begin with and a big gust of wind came down and opened the door and it banged against the wall. Well who the hell went over to the locker then? Where did the person go to when they went back up there? Did they fly off the roof? There's no where to go."

This was not the only time John's sleep was disrupted by a seemingly supernatural fireman.

"The first time this happened, I chalked it off to someone jagging me off or someone coming in who just didn't want to admit that they woke me up. So I just figured

49

'Ah, forget it.' Maybe I was sleeping. But another time I was sleeping up here it happened again.

"That same feeling of cold air blasting down the hose tower came and laid over my bed. Well, there I am under the blankets, but I heard no noise, nobody rattling nothing, just nothing. I could just sense that there was someone standing next to my bed, looking down at me. And I had that cold blast over top of the bed.

"Now I'm pissed off, and I threw the blankets over my head expecting to 'A'–find someone standing here right next to me, and 'B'–find that door wide open for that blast of cold air.

"The door was closed tight, the bolt was down, and there was no one standing by me. And as soon as I threw the covers off my head, the blast went away. I really got the goose bumps because I honestly felt someone was standing right here."

John quietly surveyed the room. "I'll wash out every other story before I believe in it ... but sometimes it scares me a little bit–I can't figure it out."

Don escorted us up the stairs to the now infamous hose tower.

The station's roof presents a sweeping view of the city, and as we looked out to Pittsburgh's bridges and byways, Don continued to drop bits of information about the station's history.

According to Dorsey, the solitary cubicle at the top of the hose tower once provided a serene retreat for men studying for promotion. Scribblings inside the tower commemorate past and present Troy Hill firemen, revealing the company's camaraderie.

"We do a lot of work to keep this place nice," said Don. "We have a lot of pride and enhance the place as much as we can, and the community helps us, too."

One Troy Hill citizen even takes it upon himself to help maintain the cemetery where many firemen are buried.

According to Don, the man says, "If I don't take care of the stones, they won't let me sleep at night."

'They' have been known to actually materialize in the fire house, causing restless nights for many men.

"We got a new guy in the summer of 1985," said Don. "I asked him how his first night watch was, and he said, 'It was great, but who are those guys?'

"I said, 'What guys?'

"He said, 'Those guys! Every time I sit down there's a bunch of guys out on the engine room floor.' He said every time he went out to check the doors and windows they were gone.

"I asked him what they looked like, and he said, 'They look like us–they look like firemen. Then another fellow came down and he said, 'They're at it again. You think they'd let you get some sleep. They pulled the blankets off me again!'"

An exact identity hasn't been assigned to the 'he' or 'they' at Troy Hill. "Everyone always kids, 'It's your father, or your father,'" said Don. "But there's so many that come through here, no one really knows and we don't really attribute the strange things to anyone in particular."

"You have to understand, something like this happens, and you just figure you'll keep it to yourself," said John. "You think someone will think you're crazy. But if someone else brings up their own story, then you feel like you can tell them about your experience. That's how we get to know other guys' stories."

John related another firemen's unusual encounter in the building.

"They used to play cards down in the basement many years ago. It was a community thing–not just the firemen.

"In the past few years, one of the guys was up on night watch, and he went down to go to the bathroom. So he walked down the cellar steps and across the floor.

"Now it's at night, no one else is here, it's quiet, and

you're not expecting to see anyone down there. There's one little light bulb hanging in the bathroom. He walked toward it, and did a double take; there was a table full of guys sitting around playing cards! He looked, and there was a card game in progress right there!

"He looked away for a split second, and when he looked back, they were gone."

Could it be the 'ghosts' in the building are the product of long, hard shifts and weary eyes? Don Dorsey and John Arnold don't think so.

Could it be that firemen once stationed in old Company #11 or perhaps #51 have never really left their posts?

Could it be that traces of the men who dedicated their lives to protecting their neighborhood still remain in the building?

The Troy Hill Fire Company is immortalized on film in the movie, "Hoffa". While probably unrecognizable to most viewers, Dorsey assured us his building did indeed appear in the film, and that while at Troy Hill, one of the picture's stars even took time to test the fire pole.

"Danny DeVito was here sliding the pole!" he exclaimed.

With that pronouncement we decided to take the pole for a spin of our own.

In the four second slide all thoughts of ghosts were replaced with a new kind of delicious fright as the cold concrete of the engine room floor rapidly came into focus beneath us.

"Next time, you have to land on your feet!" John called from the top of the hole in the bunk room.

I think we'll stick to ghosts.

●

TOMBS AND TOMES

Every Halloween from approximately 1976 to 1979, spirits roamed the musty cellar hallways of the Lawrenceville Branch of the Carnegie Library.

They would move through the dank canals of the basement, converging at last in the large room where staff members say leering countenances were seen glowing in fiery hues.

The spirits, though imbued with supernatural sentiments, were very much alive. And most of them were fewer than 12 years old. In addition to parents, freshly carved jack-o'-lanterns accompanied the children on a frightful night flight into volumes of ghostly literature as vociferated by children's librarian Kathy Herrin.

"When I was children's librarian there, I decided that we should use the basement for ghost stories at Halloween," said Herrin, now children's librarian at the East Liberty Branch of the Carnegie Library.

"The basement was not in the best condition–it has an old wooden floor, and everything is creaky and unpainted. There are stacks of old books around the room that give it a terrific atmosphere...it was the perfect place for ghost stories."

Especially considering the building has a story of its own.

The plot now occupied by the Lawrenceville branch also has a ghost story of sorts, and a tumultuous history which is chronicled in the book, *Monster on the Allegheny ...and Other Lawrenceville Stories* by Allan Becer, James

Wudarczyk and Jude Wudarczyk.

"In the months following the founding of Lawrenceville by William Foster in 1814, a concern arose over the lack of a burial site for U.S. Soldiers, especially for those stationed at the U.S. Arsenal, as well as for the citizens of the community, who found the burial sites in the nearby City of Pittsburgh too far removed from their homes."

The book goes on to state that William Foster donated one and one fourth acres of land to be used as a cemetery for American soldiers and Lawrenceville citizens: the Lawrenceville Burying Ground was born. The land today supports the Lawrenceville Library.

"As Lawrenceville grew, so did its need for a schoolhouse, and the residents soon petitioned William Foster for permission to erect a school on an unused portion of the burying ground."

According to Becer, Wudarczyk and Wudarczyk, Foster reluctantly agreed to the development provided the building be removed from the site when the land came into demand as a grave site.

Sometime between the years of 1826 and 1829, volunteers built the school. In 1834, Lawrenceville was incorporated into the City of Pittsburgh as an independent borough, which now claimed dominion over cemetery activities. The cemetery became known as the Washington Burial Ground, and fees for interment were instituted to fund the upkeep of the grounds.

"The Borough Council also voted to remove the long unused schoolhouse that still stood on a corner of the ground, which was sold for $5.77, torn down and carted away. Money was also expended to erect fences as well as walkways through the grounds"

With the conception of the Allegheny Cemetery in 1844, a decrease in burials in the Washington Burial Ground laid to cemetery to rest, so to speak.

"...[in 1868] the Borough of Lawrenceville ceased to

exist and was incorporated into the City of Pittsburgh and designated as City Ward 17. All property formerly belonging to the Borough passed into the hands of the City, including the community's burying ground.

"During the course of the City's guardianship, there was only one known burial in 1879, and the grounds themselves were allowed to deteriorate."

The Washington Sub-School District of the 17th ward was expanding at this time, and in 1881 petitioned Pittsburgh City Council to allow them to erect a new school building on the burial grounds.

The land was sold to the district for one dollar, under the stipulation that the school board "take proper and respectful care of the remains interred therein and cause the same to be interred in some other graveyard or cemetery."

Ads were placed in the *East Ender* newspaper asking loved ones of the interred to claim the bodies (and rebury them in another location.)

An area resident, Hugh Danver, was hired with a team of 6 to remove the unclaimed bodies for reinterment in a portion of the plot of land reserved for the remains.

During subsequent excavation of the land in preparation for the construction of the school, bones, coffins, tombstones and other remains of the deceased were uncovered. The discovery enraged residents.

"One newspaper referred to the School Board as 'educational ghouls', while another reported that 'there is a resurrection of bodies in the old Main Street graveyard now in progress.' Reporters wrote of bones and coffins being tossed about, among them a skull with two bullet holes, several skeletons that workmen claimed were at least seven feet tall, as well as two metallic coffins, one containing the well preserved body of a baby."

Morrison Foster, a son of the late William Foster, lead a number of court battles against the school board and the city for retention of the property as a burial ground.

In 1882 a judge ruled the building would not be constructed and the bodies would remain intact in the cemetery. The school board appealed the decision, and eventually a compromise was made: The unclaimed remains would be reinterred in a deep burial plot on a designated portion of the grounds, and a school board-funded monument would be erected, identifying the land as a gift from William Foster for use as a burial ground. That monument stands today.

The Washington Sub-School donated a portion of its land to the city to build a free library, now the Lawrenceville Branch of the Carnegie Library.

Henry Snowden, an Irish immigrant who came to Pittsburgh in 1821, saw the deaths of six of his young children, all of whom were initially buried in the Lawrenceville Burying Ground.

The bodies were moved to the Snowden Family Plot in the Allegheny Cemetery in 1882. For unknown reasons, the tombstone of one of the Snowden children never made the trip to Allegheny, and rests today in the basement of the Lawrenceville Branch of the Carnegie Library.

The stone is worn and is difficult to read. All that remains in memorial is:

IN MEMO

NRY

RY   & C

SNOWD

who departed

Dec. 7th   183

ged   1 year & 3 mon

As reconstructed by Becer, Wudarczyk and Wudarczyk, the missing letters, when added to the readable ones, form:

IN MEMORY OF
HENRY SON OF
HENRY & CATHERINE
SNOWDEN
who departed
Dec 7th 1830
Aged 1 year & 3 months

Some believe this marker retains the energy of a budding life extinguished in its youth. Some say the misplaced headstone is the physical indication of a restless spirit...that haunts the Lawrenceville Library.

Kathy Herrin capitalized on the spectral speculations. "I invited children to carve pumpkins and bring them to the library one night around Halloween—we lit all the pumpkins and judged them," she said.

"I would always pull out the tombstone, and talk about the fact that this was a stone supposedly from a graveyard that existed where the library stood now. I'd try to set a scary atmosphere, then I'd tell them that 'The spirit of the child must surely be present with us as we tell ghost stories now.'"

Herrin said the story was a favorite with the standing-room-only crowd of 200 to 300.

The library, which children's librarian Rebecca O'Connel said is patronized primarily by children and senior citizens, preserves much of its original look.

Wrought iron shelves hold books in a spacious room illuminated by huge windows.

A picture of the library's interior in its early years shows an umbrella stand that staff members believe is the one which resides in the library today.

And the tombstone of young Henry Snowden lies in the basement, a constant reminder of what once claimed the ground beneath the building, and what, or who, still may.

●

THE DEACON OF THE
DEPRECIATION LANDS MUSEUM

Nestled in a corner of Allison Park, cloistered from the bustle of commercialism the nearby Hampton Plaza creates, the Depreciation Lands Museum quietly commemorates a little-known portion of Western Pennsylvania History.

The volunteer-run operation is tiny, with a focus on education. Children are favorites at the museum, which offers a number of hands-on programs for youngsters.

For a minimal fee, the under-12 crowd can participate in any number of 11 programs the museum features, including day and week-long excursions into the past.

"Adventures in Pioneer Living" is described in museum literature as "A day camp type experience for learning about pioneer life." Costumes are provided, and participants are treated to a ride on the museum float in the Hampton Fourth of July Parade.

As a "Pioneer for a Day", children cook and eat pioneer food, make pioneer crafts, and sleep in the museum's log house.

Amidst all this history, all this Daniel Boone-ing, there's another aspect of the Depreciation Lands Museum, one that isn't a part of museum displays.

Some seemingly unexplainable experiences of several volunteers during the renovation of the building the museum now occupies prompted the editors of the organization's newsletter to go public with The Deacon.

"Has he always been here–this spirit (or ghost, if you prefer) that we call 'The Deacon'?" the first issue of the "Newydd", the museum's newsletter, questioned.

"Is he the same entity that the Indians called 'The Great White Spirit'? Was he around when James Cunningham was surveying the land–blazing the trees and pounding the stakes?

"Who knows? But every old building needs a resident ghost (it makes it more interesting), so The Depreciation Lands Museum has adopted (or invented) one. We leave that decision to our readers; but there are those who say that they have seen him–or felt his presence–or thought that he intervened on their behalf in times of danger. However that may be, we claim him, and have even given him a name. We call him "The Deacon", because the building that houses him was once a church, and we thought that name was appropriate."

Members of a Reformed Presbyterian congregation built the church the museum occupies around 1839. In the late 1960's, the building ceased to operate as a house of worship. The township purchased it and soon the Depreciation Lands Museum took residence in the structure.

Lib Hunter, an active museum volunteer, provided a tour of the museum on a damp, chilly Sunday.

She greeted us in period costume, and while she had no personal acquaintance with The Deacon to relate, she did showcase her warehouse of historical knowledge of the museum and the Depreciation Lands.

The main building in the museum complex tells the story of the lands.

With the depreciation of early U.S. money known as Continental Scrip came hard times for Revolutionary War soldiers who were paid with it. Pennsylvania attempted to alleviate the problem by purchasing land from the Iroquois Indians, and issuing "Depreciation Certificates", good for purchase of the land, to soldiers.

Indians infuriated with the decision of their leaders to sell prime hunting grounds created problems for the settlers who felt the land was now lawfully their own. The conflicts were eventually resolved in favor of the settlers after long and often bloody battles.

Reproductions of early Depreciation Lands maps hang superimposed over modern maps of the area in the museum. Collections of early tools and household items offer insight into the lifestyles of the pioneers. And cut-outs of the key figures of the Depreciation Lands depict history in nearly life size storybook form.

The oldest building on the property is the Armstrong Log House, built in 1803, less than a mile from its present location at the museum.

In December, 1973, the homestead of Scotsman Thomas Armstrong was dismantled and moved to the museum property. A good portion of the original building remains intact in its restored form.

Another museum building houses an original Conestoga wagon. The newest building in the complex is a reproduction of a one-room schoolhouse. A small cemetery, too, rests on museum grounds, eerily shaded by towering vegetation.

Perhaps The Deacon is buried in the graveyard.

"He is a crusty old character; and judging by his speech, probably not too highly educated; but no one doubts he was an intelligent and respected member of his community," the newsletter article continues.

"He has a good memory, and retains a lot of information about the people and events of the early days in The Depreciation Lands, all of which makes him eminently qualified for the position he will henceforth fill in our newsletter–that of a columnist bringing us news of a bygone era."

The 'ghost writing' taking place in Allison Park includes seasonal stories of the supernatural The Deacon has managed to scare up over the years.

The story of the volunteers' initial acquaintance with The Deacon is told in the same newsletter article.

When the church was being renovated in 1974 and '75 for use as the museum, volunteers found themselves replacing window glass, repairing and repainting ceilings and walls, and recording tombstone inscriptions for museum files.

It was during this busy work period that The Deacon was first discovered. A volunteer who was replacing broken panes of glass in windows experienced difficulty fitting the new glass into place.

Tired from a long day's work and anxious to finish the job, the woman decided to correct the problem by shaving some wood from the window with her pocket knife to create space for the glass.

Again, we turn to the newsletter for a close account.

"Now she was not a fanciful woman; but as she worked, she felt that someone else was present. She looked around and saw no one, but still...

"Then, out of the corner of her eye, she saw a man standing right in the middle of the freshly painted floor. When she spun to face him, the room was empty; but again, out of the corner of her eye, she saw the homespun trousers and the black calf-high boots.

"In an exasperated voice, she finally spoke to him, feeling a bit foolish at talking to herself–or to empty space–'Well don't just stand there,' she said. 'The least you can do is help!' And at that moment, the little knife cut exactly the right amount of wood from the recalcitrant frame and the glass fit perfectly."

A similar incident shortly thereafter involved a young boy who was painting over the stairwell. The ladder the child was perched upon tipped, and had just reached "an impossible angle" when volunteers said it stopped and returned, slowly, to an upright position.

Did The Deacon break the young worker's fall?

Many unusual events in the building have been attributed to The Deacon. He is a friendly specter, always willing to help those caring for his building.

Talk of the ghost some believed roamed or even protected the building fell to a hush until 1993, when an incident revived the wraith.

"Many changes had been made in the old buildings, one of them being a new dropped ceiling in the building known as 'The Annex.' The old ceiling had not been removed, as it was not considered dangerous–only unsightly–and the room now served as a multi-purpose area."

Many years after the ceiling replacement, a group of Girl Scouts spending the weekend at the museum had retired to their sleeping bags strewn about the museum floor, when a loud crash awakened their troupe leaders.

Some of the tiles from the old ceiling had fallen onto some of the newer tiles which in turn fell and even broke the glass on one of the light fixtures.

Bits of plaster and shards of glass now lay mingled among the slumbering campers. Miraculously, not one head was touched In fact, most of the youngsters slept through the entire episode.

"The Deacon after all these years???" the newsletter asks.

"No one actually claims that it was. All any one will say is that what could have been a catastrophe for a lot of little girls turned out to be merely an exciting experience–and we, at the Museum, are grateful for the good luck, or happy chance, or whatever one cares to call it–but we like to call it 'The Deacon'–still taking care of 'his people'!"

•

THE GHOSTLY PLAYHOUSE PLAYERS

The house lights dim and audience chatter fades to inaudibility as the excitement of the impending theatrical experience seizes both actors and audience.

The four seconds of limbo preceding the majestic rise of the curtain tick off slowly, distinctly, seductively, like the click of heels across the silent stage.

In one measured moment of anticipation, hundreds of held breaths release to propel The Playhouse production forward, and like a tightly-wound toy suddenly turned loose, the play springs to action.

But after this place of fantasy, this house of drama, falls dark and is allowed to rest, what characters continue to roam the building and its stages?

What unseen scenes are played out–what fantastic dramas take the spotlight?

If you visit The Playhouse on Craft Avenue in Oakland, you may meet John Johns, Gorgeous George, the Lady in White, Weeping Eleanor, and the Bouncing Red Meanie or the Bouncing Looney (depending on which production you see).

According to some Playhouse staff and actors who use the facilities, these characters are regulars at the theater–but you can't buy a ticket to the show they put on, for this is a troupe of paranormal players who don't schedule performances.

According to staff and actors, the Pittsburgh

Playhouse is haunted.

Many theaters harbor ghost stories. The nature of such a building readily lends itself to tales of the supernatural–the elements of mystery are inherent. Theaters are typically shrouded in darkness–daylight is a rarity and artificial illumination prevails. Lights, sets, actors–all the components of a theater–create illusion.

But while many theaters claim supernatural stories, few have the diverse history of the Pittsburgh Playhouse.

Parts of the building have been the Tree of Life Synagogue, a wedding reception hall, a bar, and, according to a Playhouse staff member, a brothel.

The personalities that comprise the theater's ghostly cast are just as diverse, perhaps perverted by time and sensationalism. Consistency among stories of experiences with the characters does exist, however.

The spirit of John Johns, a prominent Pittsburgh actor in the 1950's and '60's, is said to haunt the theater.

Johns collapsed, apparently after suffering a heart attack, during a banquet in the basement of the building in 1963. He was carried to dressing room number seven, where he died.

Story has it Johns' ghost can be heard walking the corridors which connect the building's three theaters.

Some say he also climbs the stairs leading to the dressing room–many have reported hearing the disembodied footsteps tramping towards number seven. The sounds always cease at the top of the staircase in front of the dressing room door, but never descend the flight or move on to another room.

Students using the theaters have seen a man in an old-fashioned tuxedo checking scenery and props in the oldest part of the the building, the Hamlet Street Theater, which has been used as a playhouse since 1939. According to their director, the man fits Johns' description.

The wife of a Playhouse staff member also saw a

64

mysterious man in the theater, sitting alone after a performance. She spoke to him but received no reply, and left the theater to find her husband to tell him about the stranger. Later that evening, the woman identified John Johns in an archives photo as the man she saw in the Hamlet Street.

The spirit of another Hamlet Street performer is said to haunt the theater. In the 1930's, an actress allegedly shot her husband, his mistress and then herself in the building's bar.

Dubbed the Lady in White, she has been seen sauntering across the balcony in the Hamlet Street Theater, and has also been sighted in The Theater Upstairs, which has been closed since 1976 and is now used as storage.

The *Pittsburgh Press Family Magazine* reported in its October 29, 1978 issue that a Playhouse technical director known as The Swede had an encounter with the Lady in White.

The magazine stated that in the early 1970's the unflappable director was working on a light fixture in The Theater Upstairs when he noticed a woman in white on the dark stage.

The woman slowly turned to face The Swede, and as she did, she pointed a gun at the director. The Swede was so shaken he immediately quit his job at the theater.

The Lady in White has been seen with her weapon of choice on several other occasions.

Could the apparitional actress be the same woman a Point Park College drama student saw dancing on stage with a man garbed in black?

The ebony and ivory duo was spotted by the student who had retired to the empty Hamlet Street for a rest from rehearsal.

Another spirit, Weeping Eleanor, has not been *seen* in the building, but her crying has been heard at night in a dressing room which, when opened, reveals no one.

According to a 1982 *Pittsburgh Post-Gazette* article, box office administrator Craig Eslep said row houses were once located where the back portion of The Playhouse stands today. A fire which destroyed the homes also took the life of Eleanor and her daughter, he said.

On the more sensational end of the Playhouse's supernatural spectrum sits The Bouncing Red Meanie (or Looney), who seems to be one of the most frequently-experienced ghosts in the building.

The Rockwell Theater, formerly the Craft Avenue Theater and before that the Tree of Life Synagogue, is where the Meanie/Looney takes center stage.

The *Post-Gazette* quoted Eslep.

"In 1971, on Halloween night, five Point Park students decided to hold a seance on stage. A lot of people believe that this was when the Bouncing Red Meanie first appeared.

"These students locked up the building at midnight and turned off the switchboard, a regular practice. About 10 minutes into the seance, a red figure appeared at the back of the theater and began pacing back and forth, frantically.

"Then every telephone in the place began to ring. Four of the people were facing backstage and one, a girl, was looking out toward the seats. She became visibly upset. The other four turned around to see every seat in the theater occupied by silent people dressed in turn-of-the-century outfits."

According to the *Post-Gazette*, Eslep said the students fled the theater and independently gave identical accounts of the experience the next day.

Reports of Meanie encounters are usually quite similar: A tall, stooped red man with a worried expression paces the theater. His consternation and gait escalate to a frenzied pace until he finally levitates and swoops near the theater's ceiling or even bounces off the walls—thus the moniker "Bouncing Red Meanie (Looney)".

A sarcastic wit duly named "Gorgeous George"—the apparition of a green man with a decaying face who is also said to haunt the theater. Gorgeous was reported to have rapped on the glass of the costume shop in the basement of the building, giving a young actress inside the shop a terrific fright.

Many of the stories of the ghostly characters at The Playhouse are somewhat nebulous. Many accounts are at least 15 years old, and while many associated with the theater say they know someone who knows someone who's encountered one of the spooks, few who currently work in the theater would attest to a personal siting.

At least not of John Johns. Or The Lady in White. Or even the Bouncing Looney. Or Meanie.

Lisa Phillips, a box office employee, did, however, put her own spin on the histrionic hauntings.

"There is a ghost in the box office," the young woman stated without hesitation. Phillips has worked in the office since 1989.

"The main thing it does is spin the round top—the flip lid—on the garbage can. I've seen that happen four times—sometimes, when there's been other people in there.

"The lid will just start flipping loudly...we cover it a lot now—we put a money box on top of it so the lid can't move, but then the money box will bang...so you know it's trying to flip it."

Phillips said the ghost plays tricks when the box office is empty.

"We think it opens the file cabinet. There's obviously tons of explanations of how a file cabinet could get opened when no one's in there, but all the drawers are open—and we think it might be the ghost."

While Lisa contends The Playhouse is a generally positive place to work, she said she does get uneasy feelings in the building.

The Theater Downstairs, which is used by Point Park

College's Theater Company, is, in Lisa's words, a "spooky" place.

"It's almost like a boiler room that was made into a theater," she said. "There are four coffins in a row down there left over from a show. I go down there sometimes and there's no way to explain it, but it's spooky–beyond just looking weird."

Lisa said the 'weirdness' does not subside when others are downstairs with her.

"A friend who works in the box office was doing a show in the Rockwell, and she saw a ball of light. She followed it around, could reach toward it but never touch it, and could feel the cold air coming from it," she said.

A prankster toying with lighting equipment? Phillips said no.

"I've heard so many stories," she said.

The building has gathered a lot of them in its approximately 100 years of existence.

Are the tales of ghosts in The Playhouse merely exaggerated drama perpetuated by the creaks and groans of an old building–the tired eyes of weary workers–the overactive imaginations of the groups of highly creative people that have passed through the theater?

For those who have found themselves audience to an unexpected, supernatural show, the ghosts of The Playhouse are as real as it gets.

•

SPIRITS OF THE CATHEDRAL OF LEARNING

Students at the University of Pittsburgh derive equations, conjugate foreign verbs and write poetry in the Gothic, 42-story Cathedral of Learning.

Known as the world's tallest academic building, the edifice rises majestically over Oakland, inviting students to study in the hush of the sweeping arches of its Commons Room.

The traffic of modern academia blends anachronistically with the Gothic architecture, and most students pass through the building seemingly unaware of their awesome surroundings. Only visitors gape at the building's resplendence, and only visitors register shock at news the Cathedral's Nationality rooms are regularly utilized Nationality Classrooms.

The Classrooms are "tributes to the heritages of the city's ethnic groups." University literature states they are funded by Pittsburgh's ethnic communities "and often designed by renowned architects abroad."

"A visit to the Nationality Classrooms is virtually a mini-tour of 23 nations in a time-warp that transports you from 5th-century B.C. Greece, through 1st-century Israel, 6th-century Ireland, 15th-century Italy, to 16th-century Poland, with many stopovers.

"Original and recreated furnishings combine with carved stone, stained glass, sculptured and inlaid wood to provide unforgettable glimpses of European, Scandinavian,

69

Middle Eastern, African, and Asian cultures."

Those cultures hold much allure for students and visitors to the Nationality Classrooms, yet it seems most are particularly interested in the history of American culture.

According to E. Maxine Bruhns, Director of the Nationality Rooms and Intercultural Exchange Programs at the University, the Early American Room is often the favorite room on tours.

According to Bruhns, many also say "the favorite" is haunted.

"This is a room that was done as a representation of American Culture in the 17th-century," she said.

"Theodore Bowman, a nephew of the man who built the Cathedral, went to England to find original material with which to make this room. He went to shipyards and got huge beams that are in the fireplace, and 200-year-old brick. He also went to the House of Seven Gables and designed this room with a hidden passage of its own."

The seven-foot high room portrays the "sturdy simplicity of life in America during the 1600's". The combination kitchen-living room contains a nine-foot fireplace built of handmade brick, complete with household items including a spider gridiron, longhandled waffle iron, bread shovel, skewers, iron kettles, ladles, and forks.

The room also houses two rifles, a collection of 17th and 18th-century American coins and a hand-stitched sampler.

"The room is kept locked," said Bruhns, "Because of all the valuable (and dangerous!) items inside it."

The release of the hidden latch in the small closet between the blackboard and fireplace triggers a spring which opens a panel, revealing a hidden staircase leading to a loft.

"The room is kind of a mysterious room to go into, and a few years ago some students said there was definitely a ghost that walked the Early American Room," said Bruhns.

"One year on Halloween night they sat out in the hall

70

and waited for the ghost. I don't know...maybe the spirit would have been a Salem witch because a lot of the wood for the room came out of New England..."

Perhaps some energy is focused in the hidden loft, which has been made into a bedroom. Bruhns' grandmother's wedding quilt rests on the bed.

Perhaps the room is devoid of any supernatural activity.

Or perhaps the students who spend time in the room have detected vestiges of the past and the lives which it commemorates.

On the first floor of the Cathedral, across from the information center, resides the last remnants of Picnic House, the childhood home of Mary Croghan-Schenley.

"She was really an enormous benefactor," said Bruhns. Schenley donated a good portion of her Pittsburgh property to public projects and charities. Schenley Park, the foundation of Point State Park (Fort Pitt Blockhouse), and land for hospitals and other charitable institutions were all gifts from Mary.

Schenley's father, Colonel William Croghan Jr., built Picnic House in the 1830's on Black Horse Hill, now Stanton Heights.

"In the mansion he incorporated a wonderful ballroom," said Bruhns. "He wanted her to have a coming out debut like all good little rich Pittsburgh girls had. So he built this ballroom with a crystal chandelier.

"Then, when Mary was 13 or 14, he sent her off to a finishing school on Long Island. The head mistress had a brother-in-law who was widowed. He was a captain in the English army—he was very dashing—he had long curls. And little Mary fell in love with him at the age of 14."

In 1842, Mary Croghan eloped with Edward W. H. Schenley, a man three times her age. A scandal ensued in which Colonel Croghan reportedly threatened to disinherit his young daughter.

"Her father nearly had apoplexy and even Queen Victoria in England was appalled," said Bruhns. "But then her husband became a consul in Dutch Guinea.

"There are letters I've gone to see over in the historical society. They're almost like postcards. Mary would write to her father how she would go horseback riding with her husband, and all the different things he was doing, and then she started having babies and brought them back to their grandfather. By then, he was all ready to welcome her back."

The mother of nine never returned to Pittsburgh for more than a year, however, and the ballroom was reportedly never used.

The house eventually fell to disrepair and in 1945 was doomed for demolition.

"Someone said they couldn't let this unique, neoclassical, neogothic architecture be lost," said Bruhns.

In 1955, the ballroom and a small annex was relocated to the University of Pittsburgh where it was restored and refurnished in 1979 and 1980.

The room is recorded in the Library of Congress in the Department of Interior's Historic Buildings Survey as "possessing exceptional historic and architectural interest and as being worthy of most careful preservation for the benefit of future generations."

The room was also declared a historic landmark in 1974. According to Bruhns, it is the only example of its kind in the United States.

As we entered the Croghan-Schenley Ballroom, the ornate mantelpiece and Corinthian capitals seemed to ask for a moment of reverence.

"There are people who say there are times when the chandelier quivers, for no reason," she said, a mysterious smile growing with the light she slowly brightened in the crystal chandelier.

"Some say Mary haunts this room—there's no

proof–but they say since she never got to have her coming out party, she came back here.

"It's so evocative, this wonderful time."

Bruhns gazed thoughtfully across the room, as if peering into the 1800's.

"I think Little Mary Schenley might be in the room."

•

1201 BRUCE HALL: HAUNTINGS IN THE UNIVERSITY OF PITTSBURGH

"I was truly frightened that night–the hair on my body just stands up when I think about it."

Dianne Abraham's face flushed crimson as she concluded her narrative of an unnerving night in 1201 Bruce Hall, a dorm building at the University of Pittsburgh.

Abraham has worked in the University's catering department since 1980 as a waitress and, more recently, as a catering office employee.

She is one of many waitresses who have catered affairs in 1201 who are convinced the room is flooded with natural abnormality–or perhaps supernatural normality.

"When I leave 1201 and close the door, it's a sound of relief," said a waitress who asked to remain anonymous. "I'm not a ghost believer, but it's like a huge sigh of relief, and I think every other waitress would tell you that, too."

All of them we talked to did.

The women took time from preparation of an event to share their experiences with 1201, the Penthouse suite of the former Schenley Hotel, now Bruce Hall.

And Abrahams dodged the din of a busy office and an insistent telephone to relate her own experience with the spirits of suite.

"Bruce Hall is a dorm building, except for the top floor where 1201 is located," she said. "We cater dinners and receptions there. It's a really nice room–the ceilings and

74

everything are just terrific–there's antique furniture in it, and those little goblin figures.

"In about 1982 I was in the room setting up–me and the lead waitress, MaryAnn. It was early summer or late spring, and everything was closed up–the windows and so forth–and we were the only two in the place.

"I was so proud of myself for setting up all the napkins a certain way for 40 guests, and I went back to the kitchen to get her to see how well I did–I was all excited that I did it all myself.

"But when the two of us went back into the room, every one of the napkins was laying down like a domino effect–every single one. They couldn't have touched each other like dominoes touch, but every one of them were laying down like that.

Dianne suspected that MaryAnn had moved the napkins as a prank, but MaryAnn upheld her innocence.

"She started laughing and said, 'Hmm ... so you too, huh?'," said Dianne. "I wanted her to explain that comment to me and I kept bugging her all that day to tell me what she meant by that remark. Eventually that evening she told me that she had an experience up there and then proceeded to tell me. And she was told then by management not to tell any of the newer waitresses up there about this.

MaryAnn said she was working alone, late in the evening, in 1201's kitchen when she felt a cold draft sweep through the suite.

"Again, all the windows–everything–was locked up," said Dianne. "She felt like something went past her, then all the cabinet doors in the kitchen–and some of them were very high–opened up, and then closed, and then opened up again. She'd close them, go back to what she was doing, and then they'd open up again.

"So one way or another–believing or disbelieving–I thought it was fascinating at first."

For Dianne, fascination turned to phantasmal fright.

"A couple years after that I was up there by myself around 9 o'clock at night. I was cleaning up after a party, and it was probably around the same time of year because there was no heat on, no air conditioning, and all the windows were closed and locked.

"I was just putting a few last things into the bar, when I heard this real loud noise...it was coming from the spiral staircase.

"I thought for a minute that maybe there was something open over there and it was the wind blowing, but there was no wind that night.

"I was walking past the hallway to go to the kitchen and it got really loud, really loud, like a hollow kind of noise, like a big steel drum. It was so scary that I just ran back in the kitchen, grabbed the phone, locked myself in the bathroom with the cord pulled around the door and called around just trying to find someone to come get me.

"Then it would stop, and I'd walk out of the kitchen and it would start again, and I thought, this is unreal.

"So after that I wouldn't work up there any more by myself. Then they put me up there with other people, and that was fine, but never up there at night by myself. I would never do it again."

During her waitressing years, Dianne witnessed other's reactions to the oddities of 1201.

"I was up there with another waitress, Dot, an older woman, and we had a bartender with us," she said. "We had done a real nice big dinner up there. Everybody left–it was about 8:00 p.m. We took our dinner, and packed up little trays and went into the sitting area where there's a TV and I said 'We're going to sit down and relax for half an hour.'

"We were sitting there eating and the bartender who was a young fellow from dental school said, 'I hear someone walking around up here!'

"Dot and I knew from having little things happen to us and hearing other people's stories...and she looked at me and I looked at her and we both laughed. And you felt comfortable because someone else was there. It wasn't a big deal then.

"So, we just ignored it for a while, and he kept saying, 'I hear somebody!' He got up and started walking around himself. It was so funny, because here's this big guy, a dental student, ready to graduate, and he was really petrified.

"Finally we told him, 'They say it's haunted.' He was really upset and never worked for us after that.

"We did hear footsteps, but there was no one else there with us. It was really wild."

Abraham and other waitresses said it's rumored both the wife and mistress of the man who owned the Schenley Hotel committed suicide in 1201 Bruce Hall. One reportedly hanged herself in the balcony behind the fireplace and the other jumped from the building.

According to Abraham, both are said to have been redheads. While none of the waitresses we spoke with claimed to have seen apparitions of women in 1201, some speculate the lost souls may be the cause of the disturbances.

Was it the spirit of the distraught wife or lover who followed Pat Castelli, Catering Supervisor, home from 1201?

"We were catering a reception and were cleaning up in the living room," said Pat. "I was in there by myself and had my back to the fireplace and got a really weird feeling that maybe someone was watching me. This went on all night.

"We finally left and I went home and walked in my house. We always have the light on in the living room for the last person to come in. Well, I got this really eerie feeling, maybe because all of this ghost stuff was on my mind, and I almost felt like, 'Did I bring something home with me?'

"I don't believe in this stuff, though, and I'm not afraid. So, I turned out the lights and walked past my kitchen doorway and down the hallway and I bumped into someone chest to chest.

"My children were little at the time, so it wouldn't

have been them. I thought it was my husband, so I said, 'Oh, I'm sorry, I didn't even see you there,' but there was no answer.

"I thought that was odd that he didn't even acknowledge me, and I walked down the hall and looked in, and my husband was sound asleep. And he wouldn't have time to get back in bed even if it was him. I asked him if it was, and he said no.

"Another time we were in the sitting room of 1201," continued Pat. "It's like a whole apartment up there. We were having dinner in the sitting room and heard footsteps in the hall of the suite, and you can't get into this suite unless you have a special key. We were the only ones who had the key at the time. We heard these footsteps, and voices, and it was just so strange."

According to Pat, a dining cart disappeared when waitresses left the room to dispose of trash, a fully doused log in the fireplace reignited to a roaring blaze, and items thought to be lost in 1201 mysteriously showed up after weeks of searching for them proved futile. Also, many have heard the mysterious footsteps that echo throughout the rooms of 1201.

"It's nothing bad," said Pat. "Most of it seems to be in the living room, where the balcony and fireplace are."

Is 1201 Bruce Hall haunted? The Office of Special Events which now occupies room 1200 said office personnel haven't witnessed anything unearthly in its neighbor.

Yet every Christmas, they hang a stocking in 1201 for the spook, which they've named Harriet.

Was Harriet one of the women who ended her life in 1201? No one seems to know.

But most of the waitresses who have worked in 1201 do know that there is something odd about the place.

As Dianne Abraham said, "It's just one of those little things about the University."

●

MYSTERY IN McKEES ROCKS

"I'm a theologian, and by nature that makes me very skeptical about things like this, but I also know what my own experience is," said Kim Rapczak, a religious studies teacher at St. Francis College, in Loretto, Pennsylvania.

"So I don't know what to call this kind of stuff, but I know what I've experienced"

Kim spends her weekends at her home in McKees Rocks with her faithful shaggy canine, Angel. Angel's predecessor was, incidentally, named Devil.

Besides Angel, this 30-something PhD candidate believes she may share her weekend abode with someone, or something else. The home seems to be a periodic hotbed of supernatural activity.

"My parents moved here in 1977, my freshman year in college," she said. "I had never seen the house, came home, and immediately detested it. Physically, it's much nicer and more expensive, but it had a terrible feel to it.

"The room which is now my bedroom used to be the living room. My mother and I were sitting on the couch one day when we heard my father come in and go upstairs and start running water in the bathtub. The water ran and ran.

"She sent me upstairs to see if he had fallen in the tub or something. I went up there and my dad was not there and the bathtub was completely dry. Now sometimes if toilets are broken they'll flush themselves, so I could understand running water...but my mother and I heard footsteps–we actually thought he came in and walked up the steps."

Kim said her mother lived in the house for about 10

years, and often heard footsteps and even the sound of a man sneezing in the cellar.

"The thing that happened here that frightened me the most," said Kim, pausing as if to punctuate her thought with a colon, "my mother was ill for several years and I was home visiting. I was up here doing something in the living room or kitchen, and she was down in the cellar washing clothes. I heard her cry out, and I ran down there to see what was happening.

"She was at the far end of the cellar where the washing machine was. I'm running back through the cellar and I suppose I could have slipped, but my impression was that traveling vertically, it felt like I was turned horizontally and thrown. I broke my fall with my hands, or I would have hit my head.

"Now I thought, 'Come on Kim, you're losing your mind!' My mother had fallen, she was back there laying. I picked her up, she was fine.

"We came upstairs, I didn't say anything to her, and we were having a cup of tea and she said, 'You know, you're going to think I'm crazy but it felt like someone pushed me.'

"At that point, I was really scared and told her what I thought had happened to me. I'm getting chills just thinking about it again."

Was the mother-daughter pair susceptible to communication from the supernatural world? Kim characterized her mother as fearless but perceptive. "The one thing that I do find funny is that in her side of the family the adult women are the ones who tend to have experiences like this. I never experienced anything like this when I was a little kid, but when I became an adult I seemed to develop this sensitivity."

Though "a skeptic through and through", Kim's mother apparently had a number of brushes with the spirit world.

"We lived in a house four blocks from here," said

Kim. "One year we were at my brother's for Thanksgiving and my mother went back to the house to check on something on the stove.

"She went up the stairs and turned left into the kitchen, and she saw my aunt stirring something on the stove. My aunt turned and looked at her, and moved off to the left into the bedroom.

"My mother went looking for her and it was only then that it dawned on her that my aunt had been dead for five years–it all happened so quickly she just didn't have time to think about it."

Kim has spent a lot of time thinking about it.

"I've done probably more reading about this kind of thing than the average person. There's been an awful lot of depression in this house...sometimes I wonder if the mental states of people who have lived here somehow generated some of this."

Even Kim's dogs have seemed to detect a presence in the household.

"Like I said, I always hated this house–it had a feeling in it. Especially after my mother died and my sister moved out, I really hated being here alone.

"As a matter of fact, I got a dog three moths after my mother died because I hated being alone here that much."

Enter Devil, who Kim assured us lived up to her title.

"From the moment I got this dog, she drove me crazy," she said. "She growled and snapped all night.

"In May or June of 1991, I was exhausted one night because she was keeping me awake every night.

"I finally decided, or at least I thought, she wasn't hearing anything outside, and she was reacting to something in here.

"I was in my bed and I had the pillow clamped over my head trying to sleep through her growling. Finally in frustration I pulled the pillow off my head and said, 'Look, whoever you are, go ahead and frolic, I don't care, but I need

81

to get some sleep.'

"I put the pillow back over my head, we repeated the same routine the next night, and after that, it seemed to settle.

"I don't know if it was my imagination running wild with me of if there was something that either did not realize it was bothering me, or once it realized I was no longer afraid of it, gave up."

A friend from Germany staying in Kim's home also sensed something unusual about the residence.

"I never said anything to her that I thought there were odd things in the house because you don't want to spook people," Kim said. "But when she was getting ready to leave I said, 'Ingrid, did you ever feel, or see, or experience anything odd in this house?' And she started to tell me stuff and one of the things was a very strong feeling of presence in the cellar, which is where I mostly have perceived things.

"She said she actually got out of the shower, which is in the cellar, a couple times because she felt like someone was watching her. And I knew exactly what she was talking about.

"...I just thought it was funny that I had never mentioned anything to her and she still experienced it."

The home's builder reportedly died in the basement, said Kim. Angel is uncomfortable with this region of the building. "This dog is inseparable from me," she said. "But it's very hard for me to get her to go down in the cellar."

Kim's most personal experience with a spirit in the house occurred in 1991. She calmly relayed her moving tale, never losing the touch of humor with which she peppers her dialogue.

"My sister died five months after my mother did. The coroner's report came back that it was an accident, but I sort of had the impression that it might have been a suicide.

"The night my sister died, I was in the bedroom reading with the dog on the bed with me. She started carrying on, doing her bit, but it was very unusual–the intensity and how long it went on.

"And I just wondered," Kim paused as if recontemplating her thoughts. "You know when you're in trouble you go home, and I just wonder if my sister was here that night...

"A few months later, June or July, it was a hot night and I slept in the front hallway to try to catch a breeze.

"In a dream I had, I was in the hallway sleeping and I woke up and saw my sister sitting on the steps with this look on her face like, 'What the heck am I supposed to do now?' And without speaking I understood that she realized she was dead, and she didn't know what she was supposed to do.

"And in the dream, without speaking I somehow communicated to her, 'Look, this is over now, you don't have to hang around here. Find the light and go to it.' And in the dream, I laid back down and went to sleep.

"The dream was so vivid, so real—and I'm a believer that dreams are sometimes more than dreams—it was so real that I suspect one of two things happened. Either that in my actual sleep, in my subconsciousness, that this did take place and we communicated, or, and I think this is less likely, that I did wake up, this actually happened, and it weirded me out so much that I suppressed it as just a dream."

We sat in Kim's living room, sharing Angel's affections and philosophies on the supernatural. The large pooch with the lolling tongue made continuous rounds, stopping for a scratch from every willing hand.

A glance around the room revealed a conspicuously eclectic personality: The Jerusalem Bible rested against a movie and video guide, and the "Jewish Home Advisor" took its own place on a bookshelf next to "Dog Care".

"I'm a very liberal theologian—some might even call me heretical—and I'm very open to listening to the experiences of other religions and other spiritualities and other paths," said Kim. "There are enough stories like this that occur in other cultures and religions that I think there must be something to it.

"Even in the Christian scriptures, there is a story in one of the gospels dealing with the resurrection of Jesus. It talks about when the tombs of the dead were opened, the dead were seen walking around the city.

"I don't understand why people will close their minds when the universe is so big and reality is so big."

●

THE MILLVALE APPARITION
REVISITED

Celebrity is not easily measured, and it would be speculative to say that any one ghost story Allegheny County has perpetuated is the region's most famous tale. Knowledge of the county's lore is transient and generational, and it is the exceptional story which survives to span human lifetimes.

The story of a ghostly priest in Saint Nicholas Croatian Roman Catholic Church in Millvale is one such chronicle.

It is one of the area's most published stories, and though its clarity has been clouded by time and translation, it is reincarnated almost annually in Halloween features in Pittsburgh's newspapers and magazines.

A good number of the people interviewed for this book had fragments of knowledge of the tale to impart, and "the church in Millvale" was the most common response to our inquiry for additional county stories.

It would seem the story is, pardon the expression, Pittsburgh's most famous ghost story.

In the spring of 1937, renowned Yugoslavian artist and professor Maxmillian (Maxo) Vanka was commissioned by Rev. Albert Zagar, pastor of St. Nicholas, to paint a series of murals in the church.

This artwork became the backdrop for the story of its creator's supernatural encounters.

Slovenian author and friend of Vanka, Louis Adamic, published a ten-page story entitled "The Millvale Apparition" in the April, 1938 issue of *Harper's* magazine.

"I decided to write this article, with Maxo's and Father Zagar's approval," wrote Adamic, "partly because I don't want the thing to get first into the daily press, where it might be dealt with hastily and superficially, to the possible detriment of the Croatian people and the Millvale murals; and partly to call the 'ghost' to the attention of reputable groups engaged in scientific investigations of psychical phenomena– assuming, for an instant, that Maxo Vanka's puzzling experiences while he painted his great murals were not of his own making, but were really 'something'."

Adamic apparently achieved both his goals. The supernatural-science community, though at times questionably reputable, perked up its ears and studies of and publicity about the church and its ghost came fast and furious. Adamic also scooped the daily press, which gave the story both detailed and cursory treatments.

Since Adamic's account seems the closest available to the source, it is the one to which we will turn for Vanka's story.

Adamic spends more than a page detailing Vanka's personality, focusing on his "sensitive temperament".

"He explained he had a 'touch' of what was known as 'the gift of sympathy', though he did not know himself what it was," wrote Adamic.

"Very few people had it. He attracted wild birds and other wild creatures, and he said that if he came to this grove regularly every day for a couple of weeks and brought them food, the sparrows, siskins, and wild canaries would get used to him and land on his head and shoulders, and let him touch and hold them in his hands. I had no difficulty in believing this."

The author cited examples of times he witnessed wildlife flock to Vanka and even climb in his pants pockets in search of food.

So if the birdman could communicate with the animal

kingdom, he must also be able to do so with the supernatural world, Adamic seemed to imply. A deeper read of the article reveals the author's skepticism, however.

Ghost or no ghost, Adamic was also concerned with the public recognition of Vanka's artistic achievements. He highlighted the fact the man created what one art critic called the best church murals in America.

Time magazine devoted a one-page article to the murals which have also been featured in numerous news articles, independent of the supernatural connotations they often carry.

For Vanka, those were potent connotations. Unable to contain his experiences, he related them to Adamic approximately two months after he finished the project, and Adamic recorded the story for his article.

"When I got to Millvale, on April Fifth, I asked Father Zagar to request everybody round the place please to remain out of the church while I was working inside," said Vanka. "I did not want curious people to come climbing up the scaffolding to watch and distract me and possibly fall. I knew that if I was to complete the job in two months I should need every minute I could get; and therefore, I also suggested to Father Zagar that, so far as possible, he too stay out. I feared that if he came in too often I might spend too much time talking with him; for I found him from the start very charming, intelligent, and entertaining. He agreed and proposed to have all the church doors locked every weekday from nine o'clock on, after the last Mass..."

Vanka took his time to set up the story, providing paragraph upon paragraph of "by way of further introduction". It is clear the experience was an impacting one for the sensitive artist.

"Now before I come to the story that I want to narrate to you," he said, "I should probably help you to imagine the atmosphere of the church at night, and so far as I can tell you, how I felt working in it. The scaffolding of course creaked all the while all over the church; but that did not bother me.

"For an instant now and then it felt a bit strange to be alone in the church, but only for an instant–I had no time for feeling strange or otherwise. Outside I could hear the whir of automobile traffic on the road below-hill and the clanging of locomotives and the clatter of trains in the rail yard. Every once in a while the church–the whole hill–shook when a heavy truck passed or when the trainmen were joining cars, making up their trains. Occasionally the two dogs that belonged to the parish house–a police she-dog and a nondescript hound–barked, squealed, howled violently outside. On the second or third night a sudden long sound came out of the organ in the back of the church, which startled me; but then I thought it was due to the vibrations from the motor traffic or from the rail yard.

"On the fourth night, as I say, while mixing paint and feeling rather cold and tired but not exhausted, I glanced at the altar beneath me, which was rather fully illumined by my lamp's downward flood of light...and there was a figure, a man in black, moving this way and that way in front of it, raising his arms and making gestures in the air."

Vanka said he assumed the man was Father Zagar, but noted his unusual silence. Chalking it up as courteousness on the priest's part, Vanka dismissed the matter and returned to his work.

"That night I quit shortly after two o'clock," he said. "As I got out of the church the dogs, which had been barking violently during the past several hours, dashed up to me, terribly excited. They rose on their hind legs and pawed me and licked my hands. But I thought nothing of this."

It was Father Zagar's habit to greet Vanka at the end of his work day (between 1:30 and 3:30 a.m.) with coffee and cake. When Vanka found Zagar waiting for him as usual, he questioned him as to whether he had been in the church. Zagar said he had not.

Vanka noted his next few nights of work were

accomplished without incident, without specter, and without canine commotion.

"On the eighth night, skipping Sunday, which is to say on April nineteenth, I happened about midnight to look down from the scaffold while mixing paint, and there was the figure again, the man in black who, I assumed once more–without looking carefully–was Father Zagar. His gestures seemed a bit fantastic, but I thought this was due to the fact that I saw them from above, and there were shadows ...I felt weird, cold; and, trying not to think of him, I worked furiously on the Madonna, who was practically finished...

"Awhile later I heard him walking slowly down the main aisle of the church, mumbling rhythmically. 'Well,' I thought, 'he's praying.'...He paced the aisle mumbling for half an hour or an hour. Glancing down, I saw him momentarily as he cut the light here and there that poured through the scaffolding. Then–all quiet; only the dogs were barking outside, the cars honking, and, way off, a locomotive bell clanging."

Vanka entered the parish house around 12:30 to find Father Zagar asleep, where he claimed he had been since nine that evening. Vanka immediately allayed his own concern about the mysterious priest in the church: Zagar must be a sleepwalker. When Zagar insisted this was not the case, Vanka proceeded to tell him of the mysterious priest.

"He [Zagar] hesitated an instant then asked, 'Tell me: Have you since coming here heard there is a tradition that this church is occasionally visited by a ghost or some strange phenomenon?' I answered, 'No.' 'Are you sure?' 'Yes.' 'Well,' Zagar went on, 'there is a fifteen-year-old tradition to that effect, dating nine or ten years back before I came here. I have never seen or had any experience with him or it, but not a few people say they have. Before I came there were quarrels and arguments among the Croations hereabouts pertaining to this ghost, or whatever it is. I am a skeptic as to ghosts and never believed that tradition, not really; but sometimes, listening to people speak of it, I admitted there might be something to it–some phenomenon which we don't understand. ...Do you know why you always found me here so late when you came out of the church?' 'No.' 'Because,' said Zagar, 'ever since you decided to work late I was half afraid that, alone in the church, you would have some "experience" and get frightened and possibly fall off the scaffold; and every night since you began to work except today I have stood watch outside the door between eleven and one. You never saw me, for I was outside, behind the door, looking in, keeping still, listening. My purpose was to rush in in case you cried out or started hastily to climb down.'

"I said, 'Father Zagar, you aren't crazy by any chance, are you?' He answered, 'I don't know, but I don't think I am.' We laughed again, then I had some coffee and, discussing the thing, we decided that hereafter Father Zagar would come into the church at about eleven every night I worked and stay with me till quitting time."

"By way of horseplay" the priest verbally taunted the specter the following evening with summons to appear. The jesting mood soon lost its humor, however, when the men heard knocks emanating from the back of the church.

"If you're a ghost, if you're a dead man, go with God–peace to you," said Father Zagar. "I'll pray for you. Only please don't bother us–"

Vanka resumed the narrative. "I interrupted [Zagar] with a yell, for just then I saw him–the ghost; or, at least, let me call him that–sitting in the fourth pew. I saw him very clearly: A man in black, an old man with a strange angular face wrinkled and dark with a bluish tinge. He leaned on the front part of the pew, looking up–not so much at me as at everything in general: a sad, miserable gaze. I saw him for just a moment, then–nothing. He vanished. But I felt cold all over at the same time that sweat broke out of every pore of my body. I got off the scaffold, which wasn't high for that mural, and barely managed not to fall off the ladder, I was so frightened–only the sensation I had was more than fear: something indescribable, but related to the milder, more remote sensations I had experienced on the two previous evenings when I saw him gesticulate in front of the altar."

Zagar had not seen the apparition, and told Vanka at that time he suspected it was a creation of his imagination.

The following morning, Zagar told Vanka of an unusual experience which altered his opinion. The priest heard knocks, or clicks, in his room that evening, similar to those heard in the church.

"They touched my heart, and everything in me with a long chill feeling," he said, "and though I could not see him, I knew there was a dead man in my room."

Zagar then proceeded to question the spirit as to his intention, asked the shade to leave Vanka alone, and then prayed for rest for the lost soul.

The church was quiet for the next few evenings, and the priest began to credit himself with running the spook out of the building.

The knocks returned, however, as did the apparition.

"There was another knock, I couldn't tell just where, but it cut into me like a knife. Then I saw him," said Vanka. "The old man in black–moving down the aisle altar ward. Terrified, horror-stricken, panicky are faint words to describe my sensation. 'Look, Father,' I yelled, 'there he goes–to the altar–he's at the altar–he's blown out the light!'"

The apparition disappeared with the light of the eternal flame. Parish nuns told Vanka and Zagar that in their eight years at the church the light had never been extinguished.

"The glass bulb round the flame is so arranged that it is almost impossible to blow it out," said Vanka. "No wind or draft can touch it; besides, all the doors and windows were closed...The light usually hangs, as I say; but now, because of the scaffolding, the fixture had been pulled up and the lamp stood like a huge red cup on the altar, where the ghost, or whatever it was, now blew it out with a puff of breath."

Father Zagar never saw the apparition, but said he didn't doubt Vanka's story when he witnessed the flame die just as Vanka shouted the ghost was extinguishing it.

"...now I believe," said the priest. "There is something here."

"At one o'clock we returned to work again and everything was normal," said Vanka, "whereupon we had two or three 'good' nights, as we began to call those when nothing happened. Then 'he' (we called him 'he') came two or three nights in succession. I had no watch, but when 'he' came I knew it was somewhere between eleven and twelve, standard time. 'He' paid no attention to the fact that meanwhile Pittsburgh had gone to daylight saving.

"Almost always I left the church immediately after I got 'the signal,' as I called the chill feeling. I tried to ignore it a few times and worked furiously." Vanka's attempts to block the mind of the apparition were futile. "At the end I had to go; the sensation and the situation were intolerable. I saw 'him' on each of these occasions when I stayed after getting 'the signal.' He looked perfectly mild, pensive like, sitting in the pew or moving up and down the aisle; yet he filled me with indescribable horror, with something higher and stronger than fear; what, I cannot tell you.

"This went on throughout the job–for two months. When 'he' came it was always between eleven and twelve, standard, except once, early in June. On that occasion he came earlier in the evening, perhaps at nine or nine-thirty, but gave me no 'signal.' The feeling I had was unpleasant but not intolerable.

"...'He' burned candles on the chandelier in front of the little altar on the right from the time 'he' came till Father Zagar entered the church at eleven. 'What's this smell?' demanded Father Zagar, entering. I said, 'He's been burning candles all evening.' Then Mrs. Dolinar, the housekeeper, came in too, in the wake of the priest, who told her what I had said. The two of them then inspected the chandelier; it was full of molten tallow, while one wick, burned almost to the bottom, sill flamed. Dolinarka put it out...

"This is my story," concluded Maxo, "absolutely true as I know it. I think I'm not crazy. Nothing so intense, so terrific has ever happened to me. A ghost? I think so–something, someone, that is not substantial with flesh and bones and blood. An astral body, if you like–something: Call it what you like. I know that I had an immense experience."

Adamic proposed various possible causes for Vanka's immense experience, none of which included a supernatural element. One proposal suggested Vanka's subconscious perceived the rumors of the ghost which permeated the parish, and then created the specter, perhaps in response to internal concerns of meeting the deadline–a spook in the workplace would give him "an excuse in case of failure".

To the question of why he didn't quit the job when the specter arrived on the scene, Vanka responded that a sense of obligation and fear of ridicule for abandoning the project due to apparitional pressure kept him on task.

And to the question of the personality behind the ghost, Vanka responded that popular belief was that a priest who stole money from parishioners and neglected priestly duties returned to the church to make amends. According to Vanka, most who believed the ghost story viewed it with an attitude of distant respect, refraining from entering the church after a certain hour.

"They say the thing to do is to stay out of the church late at night," wrote Adamic, "and let 'him' have the place to 'himself.'"

Intrigued by the tale, Adamic traveled with Vanka to Millvale to spend two days with Father Zagar. Adamic interviewed parishioners, nuns, and Father Zagar.

"Father Zagar repeated to me Maxo's account of the incident with the sanctuary light," he wrote. "He could not think of it as a coincidence. Both he and the housekeeper insisted that on the occasion when 'he' had burned candles all evening no living persons could possibly have got in to burn them, for all the doors had been locked and the keys–except Maxo's–were in the parish house. Joking, I accused Maxo of burning the candles himself. He laughed; he had too much to do to bother lighting candles..."

Some parishioners denied the existence of a ghost in their church, and were concerned that publicity the rumors of a haunting might generate would cast a negative shadow on Croations living in the United States.

"Father Zagar and I went into the church at midnight, standard time, on Tuesday, August seventeenth–and stayed there about an hour," continued Adamic. "I was, I think, perfectly prepared to have an 'experience'; but there were no knocks or clicks, we felt no chills, and saw nothing unusual. ... I was told that sometimes apparently 'he' did not come for weeks or possibly months at a time. The dogs had been very quiet at night now for many weeks.

"I left Pittsburgh, not as a definite skeptic or scoffer as I had come there, but certainly an agnostic. There seems to be 'something' in that church, but what it is, I don't know. I can say this: If there was 'something' to see and experience, Maxo Vanka, if anyone, would see and experience it."

Approximately a year after Adamic's article appeared in *Harper's*, a number of journalists kept vigils in the church in hopes of glimpsing the apparition.

Many of the news stories began with a lead similar to this March 21, 1938 Pittsburgh *Post-Gazette* story:

"The ghost of St. Nicholas Croatian Catholic Church in Millvale did not reveal himself to a reporter Friday night."

To the question of whether or not there were ghosts in the church, Zagar told the *Post-Gazette*, "Maybe there are, maybe not. Only I am not afraid like poor Vanka."

Zagar showed staff writer R.E.S. Thompson a photo of Vanka. "There, see for yourself," he said. "What do you see in that face? Is it not the face of a spiritual man? Is he not a sensitive man? Maybe to such men spirits come, yes?"

Father Zagar's successor (and the current priest of St. Nicholas) said he has not seen the spirit. Father Romildo Hrboka has been the priest of St. Nicholas since 1966. In 1984 he told *In Pittsburgh* he rigged the church with sensitive recording equipment and found nothing usual. In the *In Pittsburgh* article he expressed his discontent with the publicity the spook has garnered:

"The murals, I am proud of," he said. "There are none like them in the world. This apparition story irritates me sometimes because all the interviews and publicity are about the ghost, not the paintings. Doesn't anyone want to know about these historically important paintings?"

Hrboka went on to note he wouldn't doubt the word of Zagar or Vanka. The only evidence he has found to support their claim the church is haunted, however, is the actions of his German Shepherds.

"On several occasions they have acted just the way Father Zagar's dog acted when the apparition was first sighted by Vanka that night," Hrboka told *In Pittsburgh*. "They jumped and barked furiously around something leading to the front door of the church, and always on a summer evening around 11 o'clock," he said.

Most parishioners today view the story with uncertainty. "I do and I don't believe it," the words of one church member, seem to typify the prevailing sentiment.

These writers first visited St. Nicholas on a gray, soft day in November. A billboard obscured from view a good portion of the yellow brick building from Route 28, the highway the church overlooks.

Our vehicle bumped and jostled across the potholes of the working class town until the church, perched high on a Millvale slope, suddenly emerged.

Inside we spoke with long-time members Rose Marie and Joseph Merzlak who were cleaning the building. Mrs.

Merzlak said she was a young girl at St. Nicholas when Maxo Vanka came to paint the murals.

Scenes depicting religious figures, stories, and events combine with portraits of Father Zagar, Father Hrboka, and Maxo Vanka to adorn the walls and ceilings.

A pained Virgin Mary grips a soldier's gun, signifying her grief with the horrors of war. A young coal miner circled by mourners lays dying. Father Zagar, surrounded by New World Croatians, offers the St. Nicholas Church to God.

The magnificent artwork effects a sort of time warp. Outside, the modern Pittsburgh skyline rises and Route 28 buzzes. Inside, the ghosts of past and present Croatian triumph and conflict take seats in the polished pews. Perhaps it is their priest who appeared to Maxo Vanka.

•

ALLEGHENY WEST APPARITIONS

A 30-person assemblage clad in long coats and scarves filled the front pews of architect H. H. Richardson's Emmanuel Episcopal Church on the North Side.

The reverent group sat quietly, some inspecting the architectural wonder before them, others watching their breath materialize in the chill of the building.

Before long, a tall, articulate man stepped to the front of the church and warmly welcomed the mass to Allegheny West, an historic city neighborhood.

The persistent beginning of a smile quick to widen to its fruition was present on the face of John DeSantis as he spoke. DeSantis is an extremely active member of the Allegheny West Civic Council, and the father of The Spirits of Old Allegheny, the Halloween tour that turns the living out in droves.

"Tonight is a very special kind of tour—one we're sure you've never experienced before," he began, his pervasive mild manner warming the room.

"This is not a Halloween spook show, not a bump-in-the-dark, ghouls-in-the-shadows fright night. You will not encounter anyone lurking to scare you, no special effects or weird noises—at most you may spot a jack-o-lantern or two along the way.

"Tonight we're going to introduce you to the Spirits of Old Allegheny. These are the real McCoy...and although we can't promise a ghost sighting, we wouldn't be surprised if you do.

"We don't like to use the phrase 'haunted house'...

97

that has plenty of Hollywood overtones about goblins and nasty horror movie spook attacks. When we tell you about houses that have 'spirits', we mean just that. Don't assume that the folks who live in those houses find them any less pleasant...in fact, in most cases these are positive: Houses with 'good vibes' or a 'good feeling' that's linked to the spirits of people long gone but yet still somehow with us.

"So tonight is the night to keep an open mind.

"Don't be scared–there's nothing out there to fear.

"We believe you'll enjoy learning about these very special places and discovering that sometimes there is indeed more to a place than meets the eye."

The Spirits of Old Allegheny was born in 1992 out of the neighborhood Civic Council's Victorian Christmas House Tour.

"We wanted to control the experience of the Christmas tour," explained DeSantis. "We wanted the tour to be about the Christmas spirit, not ghostly spirits. But every once in a while a tour guide would start telling a ghost story associated with a house, and then the next year, someone would want to hear the story again. There were a whole set of stories people wanted to hear, and the Christmas tour was not the place for them."

DeSantis created a more appropriate venue for the stories, drafted a script and, with the support of the Allegheny West Civic Council, established the tour which has proven immensely successful.

While the tour focuses on the supernatural aspects of the neighborhood, it is also grounded in historical fact and is an educational tour which illuminates this wonderfully preserved part of Pittsburgh.

Civic Council members serve as tour guides–our group fell under DeSantis' direction. His extensive knowledge of his neighborhood was apparent as he gave a brief yet thorough overview of the history behind the eight square block region.

Until its 1906 annexation, the City of Allegheny was separate from the City of Pittsburgh. Built in the last third of the 19th century, the neighborhood embraced the area's cultural, social, and economic elite. Jones, Laughlin, Scaife, Oliver, Horne, Kaufmann, Darlington, Snyder, Thaw, Denny and many other prominent families claimed Allegheny West as home.

According to DeSantis, the Carnegies, the Fricks and the Phipps were the only movers and shakers who didn't live in this area.

The region did suffer a decline after the Great Depression, but was rediscovered in the 1970's and '80's by those seeking a pleasant residence in the heart of the city, DeSantis said.

"We were interested in beautiful streets, nice neighbors, and a good place to raise a family and call home," he said. "Same as the neighborhood's original builders."

"It's a small, close-knit group of people. It's very easy to know all your neighbors here. The social circle is very specific.

"When you look at society pages in newspapers in the late 1800's—lists of who was invited to parties, etc.—you realize that the people who lived here were very tight. Those lists were like a 'who's who' of Pittsburgh."

The second wave of Allegheny West residents have spent countless hours and dollars restoring the neighborhood. The work is evident in the immaculate streets and homes now on display two times a year.

The neighborhood has remained amazingly unscathed by crime, its preservation due in part to its physical isolation, said DeSantis. "Other neighborhoods kind of blend into one another...but in order to get to this neighborhood, you have to walk through two to five blocks of something that isn't neighborhood."

Our group departed from the church, which, incidentally, is the only building on the tour which is not rumored to be haunted.

Along the way to our first destination, DeSantis pointed out the home of Pittsburgh author Mary Roberts Rhinehart, credited with creating the mystery novel genre. The author of the 1908 novel "The Circular Staircase" resided at 954 Beech Avenue.

As we walked along Beech, our group resembled a flock of sheep—with DeSantis as our shepherd. Some timid souls clumped together, enforcing the buddy system, careful to stick to the sidewalk. Others strayed from the herd, anxious to explore this mysterious region.

Our first destination was 907 Beech Avenue, built in 1888 by Moses Liehman. Liehman's wife died of an illness in 1890, and during the year after her death, Moses kept a daily diary which was discovered by workmen behind a fireplace during restoration of the home a few years ago.

"He became quite a 'man about town'," said DeSantis, his quiet smile anticipating the group's reaction. "He saw as many as four different ladies a day, including several still-well-known Allegheny family names.

"Moses records his romantic exploits, extolling the delights of 'spooning' on the porch and using the clever phrase 'pulling taffy' in places where the context makes it clear that Moses and his lady friend were not making candy!"

Our flock released a cathartic chuckle—the evening was off and running.

Liehman sold the home in 1910, and from that time until 1969 the home was successively owned by eight single women, said DeSantis.

When the diary was discovered, it was removed from the home for examination. Since that time, four people have witnessed poltergeist activity and three incidents of apparitions in the home.

"The specter of a man has appeared only in the area of the entry hall and staircase," he said. "He has each time been dressed in a morning suit with a cutaway jacket—a style popular for a night-on-the-town in the 1890's."

Stretched necks and tip-toe stances typified the group's posture as members attempted to move inconspicuously for a better view of the home's dimly lit foyer.

"Two women had come to work in the house, entering by the front doors and locking them after they were inside," continued DeSantis. "A while later as they were on the stairs between the first and second floors, they heard the staircase windows begin to rattle, followed by the rattling of other windows throughout the house.

"The house 'began to shake' as if gripped by a violent windstorm, although the afternoon was clear and calm. They heard the (locked) outer vestibule doors open and, thinking that someone with a key was coming in, they moved down the stairs, calling toward the door, 'Who's there?'

"When they reached the foot of the staircase they could see the (locked) inner door clearly. It suddenly burst open, followed by a violent wind that blew papers and debris back the hallway toward the stairs.

"The air in the room became frigid. Then, moving slowly and deliberately, a gray shadowy form of a man wearing a hat and cutaway morning coat proceeded to stroll from the doorway back the hall, fading when he reached the mantle near the base of the staircase.

"The wind, the shaking, the rattling all ceased as abruptly as they had begun."

DeSantis paused as the captive crowd gazed intently through the windows of 907 Beech Avenue.

"And, there are several 'spirited houses' in the 800 block of Beech Avenue, plus one outdoor space of activity next to Gertrude Stein's birthplace," DeSantis continued.

While's Stein's home is not haunted, ghostly voices have been heard in the tiny alleyway between her house and the next.

As the tour moved slowly to Rope Way, DeSantis

101

continued to convey bits of the region's history and lore.

"Before the arrival of settlers in the 1750's, Native Americans had traversed the neighborhood for thousands of years. The Shannopin Tribe was based at Shannopintown (now McKees Rocks) and their primary east-west trail was what is now Western Avenue and East Ohio Street (in Allegheny West).

"The area of the Commons where the iron deer and Lake Elizabeth now stand was marshland–the Shannopin called it 'The Dark Place'–and they disliked traveling through it.

"Along the Allegheny River just across from The Point was a sandbar (the back channel was filled in the 1850's and it's now part of the shore near the Vietnam Memorial). The settlers at Fort Duquesne and later Fort Pitt called it Smoke Island because in the 1750's, Indians had raided the settlement, taken captives and burned them on the island. It was later called Kilbuck Island by the English (Kilbuck was chief of the Shannopin) and the 15233 zip code is still 'Kilbuck Station'.

"The Commons of Allegheny Town was laid out in 1787 as grazing land," continued DeSantis. "During the War of 1812 it was an encampment for soldiers fighting in the Great Lakes–some on their way into battle, others returning to field hospitals erected on the sight. Tens of thousands of wounded were treated in the four large field hospitals."

Reports of sightings of spirits in the Commons began to spread before the end of the Civil War, particularly on wooded Hog Back Hill, named for its resemblance to the profile of a razorback pig. The Hill is now part of the Community College of Allegheny County.

"After the war they erected the most elaborate monument possible and placed it on top of that hill, renaming it Monument Hill in the hope that the spirits of restless soldiers would find peace," said DeSantis.

In the 1930's, the top twenty percent of the

monument was moved to Lake Elizabeth. WHY???

A large stand of trees in the corner of the Commons bounded by Brighton Road and Ridge Avenue remains untouched since the Civil War.

Another plot of land in Allegheny West is of supernatural significance. The area bounded by Western Avenue, Brighton Road, Ridge Avenue and Rope Way became in 1810 a Rope Works. John Irwin owned the operation where men and boys wove rope and created ship riggings.

The facility created the rigging for Admiral Perry's Fleet at the Battle of Lake Erie, and after the battle, workmen claimed they heard ghostly moaning along Rope Way. The Rope Works was consumed by flames three times, the last in 1842, said DeSantis.

The voluntary matriculation of each member of the group now tromping around a North Side neighborhood on a downright cold, damp evening in search of the supernatural would surely raise some eyebrows.

In fact, an air of diffidence even seemed to permeate this group at our departure. With the exception of two jovial gents, timidity presided, and it wasn't until the cold had numbed a few extremities that the group's tension subsided.

By the time we reached 838 North Lincoln Avenue, however, the gloveless had broken down to unabashed friendliness, and the warmly-dressed contingent also shared the conviviality. Esprit de corps had conquered the crowd.

The shivering mass grouped around 838 as DeSantis unraveled its tale. The home was built in 1894 for newlyweds Harry Darlington Jr. and his bride, Constance Alden Darlington. The building was designed by Constance's father, a member of the noted architectural firm Longfellow, Alden & Harlow, the architects of choice to the wealthy in Allegheny, Sewickley, Pittsburgh and Boston, said DeSantis.

Married in New York City, the couple returned to live

in their new home which was situated just half a block from the home of Harry's father, Harry Darlington Sr., who lived at 721 Brighton Road with his wife and brother Henry Darlington.

"Constance conducted a 'scandalous liaison' for several years with her husband's uncle Henry," DeSantis said.

As rumors of the affair spread, Harry Jr.'s reputation was scuffed with the moniker 'cuckold'.

"Constance was later reported to be the model for the character of Connie in Marcia Davenport's 'The Valley of Decision'," said DeSantis, "a meticulously authentic best-selling novel about Allegheny City and the steel industry. The book was later turned into a blockbuster movie with Gregory Peck and Greer Garson."

Around 2 a.m. in the fall of 1902, a gunshot from Harry Jr.'s bedroom, the second room back on the second floor, rang through the house, waking the home's staff. The bedroom door was bolted from the inside and immediate attempts to communicate with whoever was in the room proved futile.

Constance telephoned her Harry Sr.'s home and instructed a maid to send Uncle Henry immediately to the scene, said DeSantis.

"Arriving quickly, Henry pounds and calls at the bedroom door to no avail," he said. "He finally breaks in the door. The staff, Constance and Henry rush in to find Harry Jr. sprawled in a pool of blood—a book in one hand and a revolver in the other.

"The newspapers downplayed the event, nothing that Harry Jr. 'hadn't been feeling well' and that his death was a 'reported suicide'.

"Harry's body was cremated and his ashes buried in the pauper's section of Allegheny Cemetery—a suicide normally being prohibited from burial in hallowed ground.

"Constance sold the house immediately to the Horne

104

family and moved to Arizona where she opened a dude ranch."

Our group again found amusement in the soap opera-ish plot.

During a recent restoration of 838 North Lincoln, a secret panel door was discovered in a closet at the back of Harry Jr.'s bedroom. The panel door leads to the closet of an adjoining room. The discovery of the passage has caused some to believe Harry Jr. may have been the victim of foul play.

In the bedroom, workmen removed a carpet with a dark red stain, discovering the wooden floor beneath it was also stained. "Despite sanding, bleaching and repeated chemical treatments, the dark stain returns each time in the exact spot on the floor," said DeSantis.

Folklore dictates that a recurring stain is the mark of an innocent victim. The indelible hand print of a Molly Maguire who placed his hand on a prison wall in Jim Thorpe, Carbon County, before he was dragged out of the cell to be hanged is a popular example of this theory.

"From time to time, people who are upstairs in the house late at night have heard soft sounds emanating from the first floor," said DeSantis. "They hear tinkling glasses, distant piano music, and muffled voices in casual conversation..."

The tour advanced, and DeSantis went home–his own residence, 719 Brighton Road, was the next stop on our journey!

The large stone building was built in 1868 by Letitia Caldwell Holmes, the young widow of James Holmes who died during the Civil War, prior to the birth of his first child. Letitia lived in 'Holmes Hall' in seclusion until her death in 1915. Her daughter was raised and married in Holmes Hall, gave birth to her own daughter Elizabeth in 1881, and continued to live in the house with her mother, husband and child.

"In 1882, Letitia's daughter and son-in-law died within five months of each other of influenza, leaving her to raise her infant granddaughter," said DeSantis.

"After Letitia's death in 1915, Elizabeth Donner continued to raise her family at 719 until they moved to Sewickley in 1925. From 1925 to 1956 the house was Holmes Hall for Boys, a chaperoned residence for young men living away from their families while they worked or went to school in Pittsburgh. These were wealthy, conservative, Christian men—it was socially unacceptable at the time for them to live on their own."

Our group reached the awesome structure and congregated on its steps. "During Letitia's lifetime, both her daughter and later her granddaughter wrote of Letitia's late night 'meetings with James'—she would stand on the staircase and carry on a conversation with her unseen husband," DeSantis said.

"Elizabeth Donner writes of three different times when a man 'spoke' to her at night on the stairs...of course there was no one but her to be seen.

"During the 1940's and '50's, the woman who oversaw Holmes Hall for Boys lived in Letitia's bedroom suite. She claimed on many occasions to have encountered a man on the staircase. As she grew older, she avoided nighttime use of the stairs and refused to discuss whatever it was her 'visitor' said."

DeSantis said his son's girlfriend believes she might have caught a glimpse of the man on the staircase, a discriminating apparition who apparently chooses to appear only to women!

Former residents of Holmes Hall for Boys viewed the alleged specter with affection: It seems the house mother's reluctance to venture onto the staircase at night allowed the boys to sneak in after-hours without suffering punishment. "She'd yell at them, but wouldn't leave her room to see which one of them its was," said DeSantis.

"The young men who lived at Holmes Hall during those years reported sightings of a teenage boy riding a high-wheel 19th century bicycle–usually in the back yard," he continued. "The boy would always disappear when anyone would try to go out to talk to him.

"Forty years later, in 1990, a Caldwell family photo album from 1884 was discovered in Washington, D.C. Letitia's nephew William Caldwell appears in one distinctive picture–a fourteen-year-old boy standing proudly alongside his high-wheel bike."

The boy in the photo is pictured standing in front of an elaborate iron fence, which DeSantis said is unquestionably the Jones & Laughlin fence which was down the street from Holmes Hall.

DeSantis extended his hospitality to the group which quietly filed into his home where, on a table in the ballroom, the photo album lay open to the page featuring the picture of the boy on the bicycle.

DeSantis took time after the tour to speak with us at length about the tour's homes and stories.

"I consider this (the boy on the bicycle story) to be the strangest aspect of what's going on here at Holmes Hall," he said. "Partially because it's come from so many different sources.

'We kept hearing from former residents about the boy on the bicycle. About once a year or so someone would knock at the door and identify themselves as a former resident. You could tell when it was coming because they would with some hesitation say, 'By the way...did anyone ever mention the boy on the bicycle?'

"I'd always say, 'Go ahead, tell me about it', and they'd all have the same story. I believe these are people who haven't had contact with each other–some lived here during different decades. But all across, it's the same story.

"To me the photo album was the clincher, because the last time that had possibly been in the house was 1923 when

Latitia's granddaughter and her family left, and it didn't return here until 1990. And yet all through the mid-1980's we're hearing from these visitors about the boy on the bicycle. They couldn't possibly have had knowledge of the photo."

DeSantis continued as the mesmerized crowd gazed around the home, some focusing on the grand staircase, perhaps in an attempt to spy the man on the stairs.

"When restoration of Holmes Hall was begun around 1990, a recurring mystery was the sound of sand pouring—that was sometimes heard in one corner of the kitchen," DeSantis said.

"After several such events, the section of wall nearest the sound was opened. Nothing was found to explain the sounds, but it was discovered that the wall disguised a sealed doorway to another room. And inside the wall cavity was the bronze plaque identifying 'Holmes Hall for Boys' that had once been affixed to the front of the house, along with a sealed packet of printed booklets describing the facility and its policies for residents.

"The sound of sand pouring stopped. Then three months later the plaque disappeared for about six weeks... until one morning the pouring sand sound was heard from the skylight above the staircase. There—in the light shaft above the etched glass ceiling—was the plaque."

The puzzling discovery, disappearance and rediscovery of the plaque is just one of many incidents in which items specific to the home have been mysteriously located or returned to Holmes Hall.

Again, DeSantis took time to talk to the authors. "The house was amazingly intact when we bought it," he said. "There were, however, some significant items missing. That's the weird part. They were irreplaceable...and they've been returned to us in strange ways that, if it happened once, we'd say, 'What an incredible coincidence that is,' but the fact that this has happened repeatedly, I believe it goes beyond coincidence. The way that I describe it is that the house has helped us to do this."

According to DeSantis, a newel post figure of a woman and two bronze sculptures from one of the house's mantles were removed in the 1970's. A few years ago, DeSantis spotted the bronzes in the catalog for the Great Gatsby Auction, a large and high profile auction specializing in architectural lots as immense as church altars and entire interiors of rooms.

When DeSantis traced the bronzes' travel log, he discovered they had been sold to a Philadelphia antique dealer in 1982, were consigned to the Great Gatsby Auction in 1984, were sold and went to Brussels, and were then reconsigned to the auction, where they were being sold as separate items for the first time. DeSantis was successful in bringing them home.

The bronzes now reside on a mantel in Holmes Hall, and the newel post figure, which DeSantis said screwed onto the post at the end of the staircase with a perfect fit, now takes its rightful place in the building.

"A coincidence is what that is," DeSantis said.

But there is more. In 1992, DeSantis was driving home from work and noticed a friend who is an antique dealer unloading two mirrors. He stopped to provide assistance with the huge plates of glass and suddenly realized the mirrors he held were the ballroom mirrors from Holmes Hall. "There were fixtures on top of the mirrors identical to other figures in other rooms...all the rooms have elements that kind of carry over into other rooms in the house," he said.

The mirrors had been gone from Holmes Hall since at least before WWII, according to DeSantis, who assumed their ornate style would have dictated their doom: Elaborate fixtures were at the time frequently discarded for simpler motif.

DeSantis purchased the mirrors which had resided for years in a bar not far from Holmes Hall. "I never would have imagined they still existed, let alone never split up, and were never more than a half mile from the house," he said.

"If I had driven down the street five minutes earlier or later, I never would have seen them. There was just this little five minute window of opportunity..."

The mirrors were undoubtedly indigenous to Holmes Hall. "Since the time we had bought the house I had been trying to find a matching pair of over mantel mirrors, but I couldn't find anything in the size I needed," he said. "These are very wide and tall, and it's not like a matching pair of over mantel mirrors this scale are something that just shows up."

In their absence from the house, one of the mirrors had been painted brown, the other red. When DeSantis moved them into his home, they were first leaned against a wall in the room where they were to be hung. When he returned to the room the next day to hang them, they had mysteriously reversed position, the brown mirror now where the red rested, and vice versa. Oddly enough in their new position the mirrors now faced their original mantle–when he hung them DeSantis discovered one of the mirrors was slightly larger than the other.

The toasty herd that had become our tour group in the warmth of Holmes Hall once again ventured into the night, this time to Ridge Avenue.

The group stopped at the gates of Byers Hall, part of the Community College of Allegheny County. DeSantis pointed down the the street to the site of what was once referred to as "the most haunted house in America."

It may be surprising to learn that scientist and genius inventor Thomas Edison had very definite theories about death and the afterlife that included the supernatural. In fact, Edison told close friends he built a machine to communicate with the dead. Unfortunately, he died before being able to perfect it.

In their book "Haunted Houses", Richard Winer and Nancy Osborn wrote that Edison's 1920 visit to the house on

Ridge Avenue apparently influenced his strong beliefs in the afterlife.

According to Winer and Osborn, a carpetbagger, Charles Wright Congelier, moved to 1129 Ridge Avenue with his Mexican wife Lyda and young servant girl Essie.

An affair between Charles and Essie ensued, and when Lyda discovered the impropriety, she fatally stabbed her husband and chopped off Essie's head in the winter of 1871.

"After Lyda was taken away, the house remained vacant for nearly twenty years–during which two generations of neighborhood children sang about an old 'battle-ax and her meat-ax'," wrote Winer and Osborn.

The building was remodeled to house railroad workers in 1892, but residents heard a woman sobbing and screaming, and in two years, the house was again vacant.

In 1900, Dr. Adolph C. Brunrichter bought the home.

"Keeping to himself, the doctor was rarely seen by his neighbors. Then, on August 12, 1901, the family next door heard a terrifying scream emitting from the Brunrichter residence," wrote Winer and Osborn. "When they ran outside to investigate, the neighbors saw a red explosion-like flash shooting through the house. The earth under them trembled, and the sidewalks cracked. Every window in the doctor's house was shattered."

When officials entered the home, they found a headless, decomposed body of a young woman strapped to a bed. The good doctor, however, was no where in the building.

"Further investigation revealed the graves of five more young women in the cellar," wrote Winer and Osborn. "From what the investigators could discover, Dr. Brunrichter had been experimenting with severed heads. Apparently, he had been able to keep some alive for short periods after decapitation."

Dr. Brunrichter was never found, and the house once again stood vacant, rapidly gaining a reputation for being an

111

evil and haunted place.

The building underwent its second remodeling and was used to house emigrant workers from the Equitable Gas Company, which was completing an immense natural gas storage complex–at the time, the largest in the world.

The men staying in 1129 Ridge Avenue witnessed some oddities in the home, but, according to Winer and Osborn, they assumed the American workers they had replaced (at lower wages) were playing pranks.

During dinner in the home one evening, one of the men noticed his brother had not returned from taking dishes to the kitchen. The man soon left the table himself to search for him, and in the kitchen found the door to the basement open.

Suddenly, a loud scream brought the other men to the kitchen. The basement door was still open, and the men hurried down the stairs.

"Before they reached the bottom, they froze in their tracks, for in the glow of the lamp they saw the man who had left the dining room only a minute earlier hanging from a floor beam," wrote Winer and Osborn.

"On the floor under him was his brother, a splintered board piercing his chest. Then a force they could feel but not see brushed past them. They could hear its footsteps on the stairs, but saw nothing. The door at the top slammed shut. The men waiting behind in the kitchen saw nothing. But they later reported hearing doors being slammed throughout the house."

Both deaths were termed accidental.

According to Winer and Oscar, in September, 1927, an old drunk claiming the name Adolph Brunrichter, told of the atrocities he committed around the turn of the century in his house in Pittsburgh. Sex orgies, torture, murder and demonic possession were all a part of Brunrichter's confession.

The New York newspapers headlined the case "The

Pittsburgh Spookman". No bodies were found where Brunrichter said he had buried the women, however, and the Spookman was released after a month in prison where, in blood on the wall of his cell, he wrote, 'What Satan hath wrought, let man beware.' After his release, Brunrichter disappeared.

DeSantis had another portion of the elaborate tale to relate.

"Around 1905, electrical disturbances began to occur inside the building," he said. "It had only gas connections, and no electrical wiring had ever been installed. The fame of the 'lightning house' drew more than just throngs of the curious–paranormal researchers from around the world converged on Ridge Avenue to probe, measure and study the phenomena.

"Most common was electrical arcing from one side of a room to the other...sometimes a whole room or floor would flash brilliantly like a strobe...several observers noted 'bold electrical fireballs' that bounced wildly inside the building.

"After a few years, the electrical activity became more sporadic–perhaps a few days at a time a few times a year-and in 1919 the last such activity was recorded."

On November 14, 1927, the Equitable Gas Company's giant gas storage tank exploded in a blast that shook the entire county. Surrounding smaller tanks followed in the explosion, bursting into flames that licked the clouds.

"The blast shattered windows throughout downtown, Mt. Washington, and as far as East Liberty," said DeSantis. "For buildings within a mile of the blast, windows and skylights were pulverized, plaster collapsed and furniture was overturned."

Hundreds of structures and lives were destroyed, and the city mourned for days amongst the rubble and debris of the catastrophe.

Two blocks away on Ridge Avenue, the "Devil House," the "Lightning House," the "Most Haunted House

113

in America" was obliterated.

According to Winer and Osborn, it was the only structure in the city for which no trace was discovered.

Other homes and buildings left crumbled brick and shards of glass, but 1129 Ridge Avenue left nothing–not even bits of basement walls. Only a crater in the earth marked its location.

Locals say that for years a telephone pole which later stood at the site of 1129 was continually hit by cars.

Today, you can pass over the site of the Devil House, and you will, if you if travel the road which connects Interstate 279 and Route 65 on Pittsburgh's North Side.

Allowing just enough silence for the Ridge Avenue story to cause a moment's discomfort, DeSantis turned, extending an arm to Byers Hall, the mansion in front of which the group now stood.

"This home was built in 1898 as a grand double house for steel tycoon Alexander McBurney Byers and his daughter and son-in-law, John Denniston Lyon," said DeSantis.

Alexander Byers, his wife and some of their five children took the right side (as you face the house from Ridge Avenue), and Byers' daughter, Maude, and her husband, John Denniston Lyon, took the left side of the home. The mansion was known as the Byers-Lyon house.

The 90-room, four-story structure was one of the most magnificent on the North Side's Millionaire's Row. Much has been written about the home and its owners, and it is widely accepted that a feud between Byers and his son-in-law further divided this grandiose household. Byers sealed doors connecting his side of the home with Lyon's, and relations within the family were strained.

"On the Lyon, or left side, the grand interior staircase climbs three floors and is capped by a skylight, the open light shaft of which is accessed from the fourth floor servant's area," DeSantis explained.

114

"The Lyon children had their bedrooms, nursery and play space on the third floor, along with two nannies to care for them.

"In 1902, a young German immigrant nanny fell asleep while caring for Byers' youngest granddaughter. The child wandered off, found her way up the servants stairs to the fourth floor, and eventually discovered the light shaft above the skylight.

"As she walked across the glass floor of the shaft, it shattered and she fell to her death seventy feet below at the foot of the stairs.

"The family was devastated. But the tragedy was compounded when early the next morning the disconsolate nanny was found to have hanged herself in the same light shaft high above the staircase. Written in the dust of the light shaft ledge was 'Entschuldigan Sie mir bitte'–please forgive me."

The Byers Hall story is a popular Pittsburgh ghost story, often featured in Halloween roundups of the region's most terrifying tales. Inconsistencies exist among articles, however: some have reported the dust writing as a blood writing, and the message as "my mistake" in Dutch, rather than "please forgive me" in German. The supernatural element of the story has not deviated much, however–apparitions of a child and a young woman have been seen in the home since the deaths of the child and nanny.

"Within a week, the household staff made the first of what would be dozens of 'encounters'," said DeSantis. "Some would hear a child's crying on the staircase. Still others saw a small girl there. And others saw the nanny climbing up, then down, then up the stairs repeatedly.

"These experiences have continued through several subsequent uses of the building. Students at a dance school located there in the 1960's were often disturbed by the sound of crying–several saw the young child. One dance instructor mistook the nanny for a cleaning person and tried to strike up a conversation-twice!"

DeSantis said that a woman who refused to identify herself called inquiring about the Spirits of Old Allegheny tour and lent a personal touch to the Byers Hall story. The woman said that while a student in Byers Hall in the 1960's, she saw through one of the building's higher windows a tranquil summer scene—on what had been a fall day.

The trees which were donned in reds and golds now stood green and vibrant. As the woman peered through the panes in disbelief, she saw on the roof of a porch beneath her the body of a young girl.

The woman looked away from the window for an instant in an attempt to comprehend the surreal scene before her, and when she returned her gaze to the glass the body was gone and the view had returned to reflect the autumn season.

Since the 1960's, a number of students, maintenance and security personnel have seen apparitions in the building. A university official said it is the one building on campus in which some security staff members refuse to work. The building is used now for student activities.

"During restoration by the Community College in 1989, elevator workmen reported to security that a young girl was loose in the construction site," continued DeSantis. "They saw her on the staircase four times in two weeks.

"As part of that same renovation, part of the skylight shaft was used to house air handling vents to the roof. Nothing has been observed on the staircase since the construction overhead, but two students and one administrator have seen a woman whose description fits the nanny. They've seen her outside on the veranda, clinging to the elaborate iron gate that divides the Lyon portion of the stone porch from the Byers side.

"Alexander Byers had the huge gate erected following the tragedy to 'keep out' his own daughter. He blamed her for having hired another woman to watch her daughter—a stubborn conviction that the old German carried to his grave and never forgave."

Some courageous members of the group advanced to grasp the cold iron gate while others peered through the windows, marveling at the splendor of the building.

Inhibitions had subsided, and the group, secure in its number, seemed eager for a sighting–or at least another tale–and our party hummed with conversation as we trekked to 930 Lincoln Avenue, the Thaw Mansion.

On the way to the Thaw's, DeSantis once again pumped us with background. "The mansion was built in three phases from 1880 to 1895 by William Thaw, whose wealth came mostly from railroads," he said.

"The Thaw family was one of Pittsburgh and Allegheny's most prominent–for business acumen, social activity and philanthropic largess.

"Beyond having amassed a fortune, the Thaws had endowed significant scientific research facilities–notably the University of Pittsburgh (Thaw Hall) and the Allegheny Observatory (the Thaw Refractor Telescope).

"Mrs. Thaw was the social butterfly of the sister cities (Allegheny and Pittsburgh) and a spot on her guest list was eagerly sought."

DeSantis pulled up his herd at 930 North Lincoln. "Enter the scandal of the century." He flashed a sly smile.

"Mrs. Thaw's youngest son, Harry Kendall Thaw, spent all of his time and money in New York City, living the wild party life of America's most visible and wealthy swinging bachelor.

"Harry fell obsessively in love with the beauty of the age, a girl from Tarentum who was the top model of her era–Evelyn Nesbitt. Posing for illustrator Henry Dana Gibson she became 'The Gibson Girl', the look that formed America's ideal of feminine beauty for a decade.

"Harry finally married Evelyn, but was immediately feverish to learn every lurid detail of her relationships with every man who had preceded him in her life.

117

"One of these men was Stanford White, the nation's foremost architect. White's commissions ranged from Newport mansions to the new Madison Square Garden in New York, capped by a life size nude of Diana the Huntress posed by Evelyn! Harry Thaw's anger became rage as he convinced himself that White had taken advantage of Evelyn's innocence." DeSantis punctuated the sentence by purposefully raising a dubious eyebrow.

"In 1906, Harry and Evelyn attended an evening dinner theater at the rooftop patio of Madison Square Garden," he said. "Sitting at a stage-side table down front was Stanford White."

"After ranting and fuming to Evelyn at his table, Harry Thaw rose, strode calmly across the dining area, and shot Stanford White in the head at point blank range. Holding the gun aloft he announced to the 1,500 stunned eyewitnesses that, 'He ruined my wife.'" A warm chuckle cracked the chill of the Allegheny West evening.

According to DeSantis, the ensuing murder trial was sensationalized on an international scale. Mrs. Thaw paid one million dollars to hire the best criminal defense in America, and the case made front page headlines.

"New words were coined and entered the language," said DeSantis. "The prosecutor described Harry's lifestyle as 'a playboy', and the defense described Harry's wildly confused mental state during the crime as a 'brainstorm', and therefore entered a wholly new plea for his client: 'not guilty by reason of insanity'.

"The jury bought the plea, or perhaps Mrs. Thaw bought the jury! Harry served some years in an asylum and was then released. Mrs. Thaw moved to Lyndhurst, her country house on Beechwood Boulevard, and became a recluse. The Thaw name was now infamous."

Passersby have reported a large, gray spectral mist in the shape a woman staring out from the first floor balcony. Mrs. Thaw is said to have been a big woman, and some speculate it is her ghost who has returned to peer out from the home. Art Rooney, a next door neighbor, spoke of 'the gray lady', but denied ever having seen her, said DeSantis.

Above the doorway of the home the roof peaks in a pyramidal shape. "Inside the attic the space soars 30 feet to a point, where blinding flashes of light are reported to occasionally pop like flashbulbs," he said. The phenomena has been described as a strobe light show.

As he led us to from North Lincoln to Western Avenue, DeSantis informed us the next stop would be the last of the evening. The group was audibly disappointed—by now its members were without question "in the spirit."

Again, DeSantis talked as we walked. "The next home was built in the 1870's by Francis Torrance, a prominent businessman from a prominent family. When we enter 946, notice the full-length portrait of Francis Torrance on the wall at the foot of the stairs.

"Built as a single family house, 946 Western Avenue had been divided into small apartments in the 1950's. After considerable renovation (where the two front parlor windows now look onto the porch, a big suburban picture window had been installed), the building opened as Cafe Victoria in 1992."

Cafe Victoria is now a combination restaurant and antique shop.

"On the second and third floors," DeSantis continued, "several people have seen specters of an old woman in 19th century garb and a cat—sometimes together, sometimes separately.

"On the first floor, staff and diners have repeatedly seen a middle-aged man in 19th century clothes, without a hat, who in daytime strolls outside, moving from the rear courtyard along the side of the house, up the stairs to the side door—where he disappears. In the evening, the same man is seen walking in the front hall between the dining room and the front doors.

119

"In the dining room, the staff has experienced repeated poltergeist activity: After preparing the table place settings and leaving the room, they return to find the knives and forks placed in the shape of an 'X', with one crossed over the other. Nobody else is in the building, and the doors are locked."

As if that's not enough supernatural commotion for one structure, the mischievous laughter of children is frequently heard throughout the floors, and in the pantry just beyond the dining room, several staffers have heard a male voice call them by name when no one else was in the building.

DeSantis stopped the group in front of Cafe Victoria, which respectfully refers to itself as 'Cafe Victoria at Torrance House'. Our leader asked that we remain silent so as not to disturb diners as walked through the building.

The charming Victorian ambiance and magnificent aromas were enough to lure these writers back for scones, poached salmon and antique browsing a few weeks later. Our waiter confirmed DeSantis' reports, saying he'd heard his own name called in the pantry while alone in the building. Earlier in a phone inquiry, another staff member said that ghosts were a part of every-day life at 946 Western Avenue.

Having exited Cafe Victoria, our group somewhat reluctantly returned to Beech Avenue, our point of departure. With the urging of DeSantis, members now began to relate their own experiences with the supernatural.

Slowly, Spirits of Old Allegheny initiates dropped out of the pack and headed to their vehicles.

Each thanked DeSantis and bade the remainder of dwindling group farewell.

It was an evening sure haunt every one of us for nights to come.

●

GEORGE SWETNAM AND THE GHOSTS OF GLENSHAW

Ancient evergreens and sprawling shade trees form a canopy over lower Glenshaw Avenue in Shaler Township, and cast a shadow of mystery over this quaint and compact region.

Sequestered from the post-war industrial remains that dominate the North Hills, the quarter-mile stretch of Glenshaw Avenue effects a time warp. Victorian style homes line the sloping avenue where most of the structures date to the 1880's and 1890's.

The town of Glenshaw, once called Shaw's Glen, was originally known as Shawtown or Shaw Mills, and was named for John Shaw Sr., who bought the land in 1799.

The neighborhood is populated by homes with rich histories, creaky floors and ghost stories. It seems fitting that Pittsburgh author and historian George Swetnam calls this place home.

"Certainly no name is more nearly synonymous with western Pennsylvania history than that of George Swetnam," wrote one biographer. "No one has contributed more in the way of enjoyable and informative history, with a broad, scholarly, and intimate knowledge of this region. Western Pennsylvania owes much to George Swetnam, whose life has centered around history, folklore, and drama."

Born near Cincinnati, Ohio, Swetnam graduated from the University of Mississippi and Columbia Theological Seminary with a degree of Bachelor of Divinity. He earned a

Master of Theology degree at Auburn (now Union) Theological Seminary and a Doctor of Philosophy degree in Assyriology at Hartford Seminary Foundation. His academic achievements are innumerable.

Swetnam worked for seven years as a staff writer and managing editor of Uniontown's *Evening Standard,* and for 30 years as a feature writer for the *Pittsburgh Press.* For seven years he was editor of the *Keystone Folklore Quarterly.* He has written an abundance of articles on history and folklore for numerous publications, and though retired, is still called upon to write about the region and its lore.

Swetnam has also written numerous books, including *The Bicentennial History of Pittsburgh and Allegheny County, Where Else But Pittsburgh, Pennsylvania Transportation,* and in collaboration with Helene Smith, *Andrew Carnegie,* and *A Guidebook to Historic Western Pennsylvania.*

This important and revered regional laureate has also penned *Devils, Ghosts, and Witches, Occult Folklore of the Upper Ohio Valley.* The Presbyterian minister said as far back as he was aware, his family has been sensitive to the supernatural world.

We sat in a warmly and smartly decorated room of Swetnam's grand home, where a ticking clock kept a rhythmically soothing yet eerie pace. The otherwise silent building exuded charm, and it would have been difficult to imagine Swetnam any more at home in any other house. He appeared an integral a part of the setting.

The home was built in 1885 by James B. Kirk, general auditor of the Baltimore & Ohio Railroad. Swetnam and his wife purchased the home in 1950.

"When the Pennsylvania Railroad wanted to build a railroad from Pittsburgh to Washington, Pa., the farmers wouldn't sell them the right of way because they were angry that the Pennsylvania, which controlled the politics of the area at the time, had blocked a railroad that was planned from

Greensburg down to little Washington," explained Swetnam.

"Suddenly, James B. Oliver announced that he wanted to build a railroad from Pittsburgh to Washington. The Pennsylvania Railroad didn't do anything to block him, and the farmers had no objection to selling him the right of way.

"He built the railroad, and all of a sudden it was theoretically bought by the Pennsylvania, who, of course, had been financing him all the time.

A similar scheme developed into the Pittsburgh portion of the Baltimore & Ohio Railroad. According to Swetnam, the B&O sent James B. Kirk to Pittsburgh to inconspicuously monitor the work they were secretly funding.

"Kirk came down here to look for a place to stay where he wouldn't be too prominent and nobody would notice him being around much," said Swetnam.

"He met up with the Shaw family here and liked them very much, so much that he wanted his wife to bring their two daughters and come over here. In order to do so he had a master carpenter copy her girlhood home in Baltimore–and that's this house."

Kirk's signature, scrawled on a window with a diamond, commemorates the home's original owner.

"The only two who have seen ghosts in here were my sons, George Jr. and John," said Swetnam. "When George was 12 or so, not too long after we had moved in here, he said, 'Dad, was there ever a Revolutionary War veteran that lived in this house?' I said, 'No, it couldn't have been because it wasn't built until they were all dead.

"I asked him why he was asking me that, and he said, 'Well, sometimes when I wake up at night there's a man standing there,' and he indicated just a little from the foot of the bed. 'There's an old man standing there,' he said, 'and he'll take a step toward the foot of the bed, look out the window, and disappear.'

123

"I asked him to describe him, and the description was a long Prince Albert coat, just like that of a business man of the 1880's or so. It sounded as though it might have been James B. Kirk."

Swetnam's son John was more reluctant to discuss his experience in the same bedroom. "Once when somebody was talking to me about it, they asked me if I had ever seen the ghost," said Swetnam. "I said, 'No, nobody had ever seen it except the ones that slept in the room—only George and John have.'

"John was standing right there, and the fellow asked me if John had ever seen it. I said, 'Have you, John?' and he said, 'I've seen it'. But the way his mouth clipped shut I knew there was no use in questioning further—I knew I'd never get another word out of him."

Swetnam also had unusual experiences in the home. Shortly after his family moved into the home on Glenshaw Avenue, George Swetnam found himself alone on a hot weekend afternoon.

"My wife had taken the kids somewhere, and I had taken a bath and was toweling myself off in the bathroom adjoining the bedroom," he said. "There was no wind, nobody in the house, nobody near. The door in the bathroom wouldn't swing lightly—it was a heavy door—but I was standing there when the door opened from the bedroom. Before I thought, it just came to me to say, 'Miss Mattimer, that isn't nice!' and the door swung back shut!

"When we were living in the South Hills in the mid-1940's and the kids were quite small, they started talking about a Miss Mattimer. When things were missing, it was always blamed on Miss Mattimer," Swetnam explained.

Perhaps it was Miss Mattimer who spoke to Swetnam in 1992. "I was in the bedroom, standing by my closet door," he said. "I was getting dressed and considering which of two neckties to put on, and was having a little struggle deciding which was which."

124

Again, the house was empty. "I finally made my decision and put one of the ties down, and a voice, a woman's voice that I had never heard before, said as plainly as you talk to me here, 'That was the right decision'." Swetnam said he wonders if the fashion conscious spook is the same one who opened the bathroom door.

"I hear sounds around the house, but I'm never quite sure what they mean," he said. "I'll hear someone knocking at the door, but there's no one there ... things like that ..."

Swetnam's is not the only home on lower Glenshaw Avenue in which residents hear things. Some say it's merely the house settling—old wood expanding and contracting. Others believe there's more to the noises.

In one home, the spirit of an illegal alien who lived in the house as a servant is said to haunt the attic.

Another house in the area is where an apparition of a tall woman wearing a long, gray dress with a tight belt has been sighted. The woman usually appears in daylight.

This historic strip of homes seems a likely place for paranormal activity. In the words of George Swetnam, "There is every reason there would be ghosts here."

•

OBIE

Firemen are intimately acquainted with the precariousness of life. They risk their own lives to protect the property and life of others and are trained to deal with emergency situations in which death is a very real and familiar element.

Perhaps it is this relationship they form with mortality that has led at least a dozen members of the Elfinwild Volunteer Fire Company to the conclusion that the spirit world is alive, so to speak.

Like the staff of the Troy Hill Fire Company, the Elfinwild members seem an unlikely bunch of believers in the supernatural–these are primarily no-nonsense, gutsy souls. Some of them don't believe the stories–and make that fact very clear. Some scoff, some say none of it's grounded in reality, some simply say, "You're crazy!"

But other members unequivocally support the belief that something or someone haunts the hall, adhering to the 'I know what I experienced' philosophy.

Over strains of "B-4" bingo babble drifting from the hall below us, our small group sat in the club room and two willing firemen relayed their experiences.

"It was about, oh, I'd say a good two months after I joined here–I would say that was in early November," said Bill Langer, a long-time firemen at Elfinwild.

"I'm laying up here on the couch watching TV. I was the only one here and it was approximately quarter to nine. I heard the back door to the old club room open and I heard feet tearing up the stairs like one of our members does all the

126

time. I'm thinking it's him and I'm waiting–he's going to come in the room and scare me, I thought. So I'm waiting and waiting, and nobody comes in."

Bill crept into the hallway and found most of the other rooms on the second floor locked. He inspected the unlocked rooms, and eventually made his way around the entire floor. The place was empty.

"I looked out the back windows, and mine was still the only car in the lot. I came back to the front windows and I couldn't see anybody. Then I heard the engine room door open, and then it stopped and I heard it click shut...I know I heard it. I stood there and held my breath–my heart was really racing at this point–I was thinking that somebody was really trying to get me–and it was working!

"I looked at the clock, and it said ten minutes to nine. I crept down the stairs as quiet as I could, and I flipped on the light and nobody was there. I went outside all the way around the building, thinking I might catch someone, but there was still nobody. Keep in mind you can't get in without a key–every door is locked from the inside.

"I went back up to the club room, looked at the clock again and it had stopped at ten of nine–that was a good five minutes I spent looking around, but it was still ten to nine.

"I didn't know what to do. I crept in and sat in the engine room, then I heard a door creak–you can hear a certain creak in the door when you go through the bingo hall. I went in there–I ran as fast as I could–but there was nobody there.

"I went across the hall, down the stairs, through the bar, back up to the top, through the engine room, back up the stairs, and looked at the clock which had now started again–it was now nine o'clock.

"I sat up here and waited and waiting until I heard something else. The next thing I heard–I know I heard–was the engine room doors open. I flew down the stairs and they were closed, and I'm like, 'I'm getting out of here! I am really getting out of here!'

"I called our chief, Tim Phillips, and I said, 'What is going on around here?! I think I'm going nuts!' I told him what happened and he just started laughing. He said, 'You're probably not imagining it.'"

Phillips told Bill that two men had fallen asleep on the couches one evening. One of them woke up to the distinct sound of two other people breathing heavily in the room. He held his breath, yet still heard the sounds of two men breathing.

When its time to assign an identity to the spook, the members say it's Ralph 'Obie' Obenauf, a former chief.

"Obie was the boss of this place," said Paul Golembiewski, another fireman convinced Elfinwild is haunted. "He became chief in the 1950's. He was emperor of this place for so many years–he was always the utmost authority–so anytime anything strange happens, some people say it's Obie.

"In the 13 years I've been here, I've witnessed things," he said. "A couple of months ago I was here and there were a bunch of guys here and they left, and the same thing that happened to Bill happened to me. It's like, what do you do? You look out and you'll see no other cars in the parking lot, then it's like, 'Well, time to go home now!'

"The living is going to hurt you, not the dead–I'm a firm believer in that. But I do believe in ghosts."

The most common and no doubt frustrating disturbance members experience is the phantom fireman–doors open, doors close, footsteps thunder up the stairs–their creator is no where to be found.

Chuck "Nook" Coyle and William "Jake" Jackson both believe there is something strange about the building. Both men have heard the invisible intruder, who seems to most frequently visit the company after 11:00 p.m.

"You get a strange feeling up here at night," said Paul. "Like you're being watched," Nook added.

"This is an escape for many guys up here," Paul said.

"Girlfriends, marriage, anything–you come up here to get away. You'll be sitting up here later in the evening and feel really strange–something is just not right. For as many people as have experienced it, there has to be something to it. Even Tim Phillips, our chief, he doesn't believe in ghosts but he can't even explain it. There's just too many strange things."

Members Tom Price and John Rihn maintain a skeptical stance. "Soon you'll be seeing ectoplasm coming out of the ceiling," called Rihn as he passed through the room.

"Nah, that's over on the couch," jested Paul, indicating a slumbering member.

"This past year we had a Halloween party," he continued. "Everybody had a good old time, but it was getting late, very late, we're talking four or five in the morning. Just about everybody had gone home, we turned the lights out in the hall, and we decided to just go upstairs and go to sleep.

"The one girl who was downstairs was trying to get a couple things cleaned up, and she went into our tool room, which is downstairs in the oldest part of the building. The door, which is a very heavy, not off-set or off-weighted door, suddenly closed behind her.

"She was so scared she panicked. She ran into the next room, jumped on top of a tool chest, popped the screen in a window, slid the window and jumped out the window in the back parking lot.

"The door was all the way shut–and it takes a lot of force to shut it. There was nobody else downstairs besides me, and nobody else shut the door. I was just two rooms away from her."

Obie again? Some of the men think they've seen the image of the chief in the driver's seat of a fire truck. Some say it's a reflection. Other members have smelled a pipe when alone in the building–a smell which accompanied Obie through life. The chief is, incidentally, buried directly across the street from the fire company in the Mt. Royal Cemetery.

The lights in the fire hall are often found mysteriously burning. "John Logan, our ex-president, lives right here behind the hall," said Paul. "One night he shut out all the lights and left to go home. He went in his house, up the stairs and into his bathroom. He looked out the bathroom window which overlooks our parking lot, and saw that the lights were back on. We have no electrical problems here.

"At our monthly meetings, we often talk about conserving electricity–everything in here–the sirens, etc.–is electric. So we always try to turn the lights off, but they're always on, and we just don't know why. All the guys who go by here in the morning on their way to work see the lights on.

"We're very proud of this organization, this is what we do...we don't get paid for this. We all take care of this place, so why are the lights on? It's pretty bizarre."

Sitting with Paul, Bill, Nook and Jake it was difficult to discount the stories the men shared. They treated the subject with their typical levity, yet moments of seriousness crept into the conversation.

"I never believed in ghosts before, but I do now–without a doubt," affirmed Bill.

"If you spend any time at this place, you experience it," chimed in Paul. "Around here, I don't think people are really afraid anymore, just startled."

Nook shifted in his chair. "You gotta be a little nuts to do what we do anyhow!"

•

STEEL MILL SPIRITS

Rich descriptions of smoke-choked air and fiery vats of productivity that once epitomized Pittsburgh are prolific. Much has been written about the steel years–its booms and its busts, its boons and its banes.

And while it's certain the smog which hung low and characterized the city's skyline was a negative aspect of the area's industry, some looked affectionately upon the soot as a sign of prosperity.

"I adored growing up in Pittsburgh...I loved the adventure of the city," said acclaimed Pittsburgh author-historian David McCullough at the Ninth Pittsburgh Writer's Conference in 1985. "I loved World War II in Pittsburgh. Every night the sky was blood red and those mills were going and you knew you were someplace. You knew your city counted, and there was such purpose in everything everybody did."

The mills employed thousands of county residents who toiled in sweltering, hazardous conditions. Many lives were lost in the industrial process, and consequently many ghost stories were born.

The spirit of a worker incinerated in a ladle of molten steel was said to haunt Jones and Laughlin Steel Corporation's Two Shop at the Southside mill complex from 1922 until its demolition in 1960.

The story goes that in 1922 Jim Grabowski tripped over a rigger's hose and fell to his death in the ladle. After his passing, his pained cries for help were heard throughout the shop, followed by maniacal laughter.

131

A *Pittsburgh* Magazine article about the haunting included a poem written by Grabowski's coworkers:

When you're walking up through
Two Shop
You'll know someone is around
If you hear a sort of clanking
And a hollow moaning sound
For the ghost of Jim Grabowski
Who was killed in '22
Must forever walk through Two Shop
Which I will explain to you.
Jim fell into a ladle,
And they couldn't find a trace,
So they couldn't take the body
To a final resting place...
Yes, there in a ghost in Two Shop;
I have seen this specter twice,
And you'll stay away from there at night
If you heed my advice.

Approximately 40 workers died at J&L Steel's Two Shop. When a man fell into a ladle he was immediately liquefied, and the polluted steel was then buried or dumped in a vacant lot. Eventually, rather than waste an entire ladle, workers would commemorate the dead man by skimming a small portion of steel from the ladle and presenting it to his family in a nugget form.

During excavation for Four Shop, some of the tainted steel was found and broken up for scrap. This process was said to have disturbed and released the spirits of the men who died in the mill, returning them to the scene of their deaths inside Two Shop.

Another spirit haunts U.S. Steel Corporation's Edgar Thomson Works in Braddock.

According to a 1980 Pittsburgh *Post-Gazette* article, the spirit first appeared in February, 1967, during the midnight to 8:00 a.m. shift at the No. 16 boiler. The boiler soon became the spirit's favorite haunt.

A thick cloud of steam was said to precede the faceless apparition which levitated about seven inches from the ground. The workers donned the spirit "The Hamburg Ghost"–they said he used to haunt Old Hamburg Road near the mill.

"Legend has it that the ghost's wife was murdered on Hamburg Road, and he was so despondent that he committed suicide by jumping in front of a train," wrote Vicki Jarmulowski, *Post-Gazette* staff writer. "His head was severed, and he returned to the road where his wife met her untimely death."

Another theory says the man who haunts No. 16 committed suicide by jumping into a ladle in the mill. According to Jarmulowski, others claim it is the spirit of Joe Magerac, a Paul Bunyan figure who supposedly worked at the mill.

A mill employee said she's heard stories of a ghost in the Union Tunnels that run under Braddock Avenue. She asked to remain anonymous, saying management doesn't look favorably upon the rumors of the hauntings. "They say the ghost in the tunnels was an old paymaster who died in an office in the plant," she said. "They closed the tunnel off, and he hasn't been seen since."

"I have a friend who actually saw another ghost here, too," she said. "A man was working on the Union Railroad which runs through the plant. He was backing cars up and called for the engineer to stop the cars, but the engineer didn't hear him and he was literally cut in half.

"My friend was down there where this happened one day and the power went off on a forklift he was operating and his flashlight quit.

"All of a sudden the apparition of this man

appeared–he was wearing coveralls and an old cap and was carrying a lantern. My friend could see his body, but the bottom half of him was all a green haze.

"Every now and then it gets really really cold right there in the spot where the accident happened..."

In his book, *Devils, Ghosts, and Witches, Occult Folklore of the Upper Ohio Valley*, George Swetnam wrote about Slag Pile Annie.

A University of Pittsburgh student working at one of the large area mills during the summer in the early 1950's encountered the wraith.

"His particular job was to run a motor 'buggy' through a tunnel under the steel furnaces after they had been drawn, and gather up the hot slag from the furnaces in the hopper cars in his train," wrote Swetnam. "After he had gathered a load he would drive his train out on the dump and deposit the slag.

"One day as he was driving his slag train below the furnaces he noticed a woman standing beside the track a short distance ahead of him. She was dressed in coarse clothes and wore a red bandanna tied over her hair."

The student warned the woman of the dangers of the tunnel.

"You're likely to get killed down in this place," he said.

"I can't get killed. I'm all ready dead," she replied.

The student immediately informed his boss of the encounter. When the young man described the woman to the foreman, the foreman identified her as Slag Pile Annie, a woman who, during the war, ran the same train the student was operating.

Annie had been killed in an accident in the tunnel five years prior to her conversation with the student.

•

MARY WOHLEBER AND THE SPIRITS OF TROY HILL

"A house can't be as old as these old houses in Pittsburgh in the older neighborhoods without some life being left in them. I have no doubt at all that after I'm here–it'll soon be 50 years–that some of me will be here. It has to be–just in the walls. Something of you stays."

This is Troy Hill citizen Mary Wohleber's case for the supernatural. The 78-year-old Landmarks Store employee and community historian said the ghosts in her home give her a sense of security. She loves her home and her city, and has been actively helping to preserve and promote Pittsburgh for years.

Mary founded the Troy Hill Citizens Inc., was instrumental in having many sites on Troy Hill declared Historical Landmarks and has written many articles about the city and her neighborhood.

She's served on the boards of numerous historical and civic organizations and is a strong presence in her community.

"She's our historian and a great humanitarian," said fellow Troy Hill resident Pinky McGlothlin. "And she's so spry–she's 70-going-on-20."

A cluttered calendar on Mary's wall marking lecture dates–lectures she would give–verified Pinky's assessment.

"I know there's someone walking around upstairs and if I'm upstairs sleeping I know there's someone up in the attic," said Mary in an accent which isn't Pittsburgh so much

135

as Troy Hill. Pinky shares the same lilt.

"I can hear them shuffling around–and it is not a squirrel or anything like that–I've had roofers tell me there's no infestation of any kind in my attic.

"One time my brother-in-law stayed here in the house alone. When I came into the home the next morning, all he said to me on the way out was, 'Don't you ever dare ask me to come back and spend the night in this house again.'

"See he wasn't used to all the noises, and evidently that upset him and disturbed him and he told my sister, 'I was awake almost all night. I was so aware that someone else was in the house besides me.'

"He even got up and went through the house...he was so positive that there was someone besides him. He heard creaking stairs and was sure there was someone in the attic."

The historian's classy home has a slightly surreal look vaguely reminiscent of a fun house–there are few right angles in the building. "Everybody goes crazy when they work in this house," said Mary. "You can't take a ruler and have a straight line–nothing is square–it's awful. But, I think it's neat." It seems to be just one more unusual thing about the home that Mary cherishes.

So who is walking around in the attic?

"We're the fourth owner, and the house is more than 100 years old," said Mary. "When we bought the house I traced the deed. There was one signature lacking–the daughter of the person who built the house. In 1944 she was 82 years old. I talked to her then and she said her mother died at the foot of my attic steps. She must have fallen down the steps–they're very steep and curved. They found her with a broken neck.

"I figure she's still up there looking for whatever she was looking for when something called her down. The woman told me what a kind lady her mother was, and so I never felt bad about her being here."

The sun-flooded home is situated near a cemetery,

another oddity about the place that Mary enjoys. "It's like living near a park," she said. "It's macabre in a way, but in another way it's very reassuring."

"I've worshipped in India, Sri Lanka, Nepal, Egypt–now there's a land where there's spirits! I've worshipped everywhere I go. I don't think it makes any difference–people have to believe–they have to have a crutch." This seemed at first an unlikely statement for a woman chosen as Teacher of the Year in the Catholic School System in 1972, but the more one speaks with Mary, the more apparent her catholic attitude becomes.

She continued with the story of another spirit which resides in the home.

"I had friends for dinner about eight years ago. Jim, one of my friends, was sitting at the head of the table where my husband usually sat. We were eating our dinner and Jim looked toward the library here and looked back out and sat there for a while and I said, 'What's the matter?'

"He said, 'Is there anyone else you're expecting?'

"I said, 'Well, no, we all ready started eating dinner.'

"He said, 'Well, there's a man standing in the library.'

"I said, 'Jim, why would he be standing there? Tell him to come in.'

"He looked and he said he was gone. He described him and it was my husband who had been dead for more than 10 years. And he had never seen my husband. He said, 'I saw him, Mary! Why would I lie?'"

Mary's tone turned tender. "You know, after Alan, my husband, died, I had trouble...you can't sleep beside someone for 40 years and not miss them. So, I was sleeping down here.

"I brought a cot down here and every night I'd roll it into a different room. My kids didn't know what to think of me! I said, 'Well, I've got to take my time.'

"I slept in that room, too many memories, so I slept in this room, but that was his favorite room. The kitchen?

137

Nah. So, I ended up out in the hallway. Finally a couple months after he was dead, I thought, 'This is stupid, I'm going to go upstairs to the bedroom.'

"Do you know that when I walked in that room...I sensed him. I don't know how to say it, but I smelt him. That's a terrible word to use, but I smelled him. And a cry, without me even being aware of it, just came up and tore at me, just tore at me.

"You know what? I sold the furniture and I haven't slept in that room since. I don't like to go up there, so maybe it's me now rather than him."

"Did Alan die in the home?" this writer inquired.

"Oh yes," said Mary, leaning forward, taking obvious advantage of the dramatic moment, "Right where you're sitting."

I was momentarily unnerved, and Mary and I vied for the widest grin during the brief period of silence which followed her response to my question.

"I was standing here showing him my New Year's Eve dress," she continued. "It was Thanksgiving.

"He must have known, because he said, 'There's some things I want to tell you.' He told me about two people he owed money to, what to do with our farm, etc.'

"I said, 'Alan, don't worry about that–that's all next spring.' I couldn't understand why he was concerned about next year.

"We always went out for a big deal on New Year's Eve, so I was holding up my dress to show him. I looked up and he was just like you, sitting here, but he had his head back and I thought, 'All be damned, he fell asleep when I'm talking to him!' And then I looked at him. He didn't even gasp, nothing. Just cardiac arrest. He died in the space of a heartbeat.

"My mother died just three weeks before, and they didn't like each other. We said, 'Won't it be something when they meet up there in heaven!' Do you know that the day of

Alan's funeral we had the worst thunderstorm in the world! So we said they must have met!

"But see, I think there is an essence everywhere, in every house, there is life that remains.

"Maybe Alan appeared that day during dinner because he didn't like it because all my guests were men. I've always felt that's why he was here–just to let them know that he was here–because he was always that way. When I was younger, men liked me, and Alan was always just a solemn presence. He wouldn't say anything, he'd just walk over and stand there. So I think he didn't understand why these men were here in the house after he was gone. Now he understands that they're my friends."

Mary Wohleber has traveled around the world, yet she returns to her beloved Troy Hill in Pittsburgh.

"I've never seen a city yet that I would pick over Pittsburgh," she said. "Three rivers, these hills–these beautiful, beautiful hills. Where else are you going to go? Everything is here for us in Pittsburgh.

"I've seen the Wonders of the World, but I wouldn't want to live there. For living, Pittsburgh can't be beat."

Even those who *aren't* living seem to agree.

•

MAUDE, CLAUDE AND THE HAUNTED CHATHAM COLLEGE

Possibly the most picturesque college in Pittsburgh, Chatham is characterized by beautifully manicured rolling hills and lawns, flowering gardens and Georgian-style buildings.

Founded in 1869, this elegant women's college tucked away in Shadyside exemplifies the neighborhood's name. Giant trees line Woodland Road, the campus's main thoroughfare, enhancing the lush, sumptuous atmosphere of the bucolic college.

It is easy to pass by Chatham and beunaware of its existence. Mere feet from Fifth Avenue, yet concealed from the street's activity, students live and work in mansions once home to Pittsburgh's elite. Historic buildings dot the campus and the rustic serenity which permeates the sprawling property belies the college's city location.

It is in this college community–in these great homes–that students have experienced the spirits of Chatham College.

Some, like college archivist Professor John Cummins, lay the stories to waste. Cummins, who was extremely helpful in providing historic background of the school, thinks the stories are "all malarkey".

"It will be forty years I've been at this institution," said the mild, congenial professor. "When I was a young instructor, I heard everything. When I was an associate instructor, I heard less. When I was a full professor, I heard

140

almost nothing. To tell you the truth, I think the students have invented most of the stories."

The dubious Cummins is nevertheless a favorite among students who believe their campus is a haunted one–in fact, they pointed to the professor, citing him as a valuable source.

"There are so many people here who tell stories and you know they're not telling them to get attention, because they're normally shy people," said Lydia Sosa, a freshman at the college.

"If you mention to someone that you've seen something, then they'll tell their own story, but usually we don't tell too many people, because if you know the stories beforehand, maybe you'll start imagining things," chimed in Heather Hines, a senior communications and music major.

"I didn't know most of the stories until last year and this year, because that's when I started having experiences of my own," she said. "All of the homes are very old, and usually you don't *want* to know about it."

We sat in a study room of Woodland Hall, one of the buildings the women believe is haunted. Throughout the evening, students dropped by and shared their own experiences with the supernatural inhabitants of the college.

According to Heidi Clark, a junior art history major, the Blue Lady takes residence in Woodland. "A girl that I lived with here was laying on her bed one night and said she saw a lady in a blue dress above her bed," said Heidi. "She had no idea that Woodland had a ghost. She told someone the next day about it, and then they told her about the Blue Lady...

"No one seems to know who the Blue Lady was or why she is here in Woodland Hall," she said.

Heidi and Heather seem to be especially susceptible to communication from the spirit world. Both women have had profound experiences with the supernatural at the college, in particular, in Woodland Hall.

"One night in Woodland I woke up and was trying to go back to sleep," said Heidi. "I heard these little kid voices out in the hall, and I was like, 'that's weird'. They were like, 'Come on, come on, let's play, let's play.' And there was an older girl with them in her early 20's, like maybe 25, and she's said, 'Shhh...come on, we've got to go.'

"Everything got quiet. I was laying on my side on these big captains beds that we had that set up really high. You know how you can hear different voices projecting from different parts of the room? I could hear this little boy in my room. And he starts laughing, and he's giggling and chuckling around and stuff...and you know when you're sitting on a bed or a couch or something you can feel if someone sits down because the cushion sinks in? Well, I felt the end of my bed sink in and I was wide awake. I felt him grab my ankle and pull himself up on my bed and he scooted up behind me and starting pushing on me like, 'Come on, come on, let's play.'

"I could get anything out–I was trying to speak but I couldn't–I was so terrified! He moved up closer and started pushing on my shoulder and was saying, 'Come on, I want to play!' Then I got up and he started pulling on my hair.

"I screamed my head off, 'Get away from me!' and I heard him start to cry and he got off the bed, and went away."

Though Heidi experienced what seemed to be a very real child in her room, she never saw the boy.

"I didn't say anything to my roommate the next morning because I didn't know *what* she thought," Heidi said. "I took a shower and was putting lotion on my legs and saw this huge bruise on my ankle. I thought of everything, and there was absolutely nothing I had done that would have caused a bruise like that."

The evidence pointed to the possibility that a rambunctious youngster had indeed entreated Heidi 'to play'.

"I don't know how, but I sensed that he was blond with a blue eyes and had a bowl haircut," she said. "He had

142

on little knickers, socks that come up high, loafer shoes, suspenders and a little black jacket with a tie."

None of the other students seem to have encountered the munchkin, but perhaps he is the same wraith who haunts Heather's room in Woodland Hall.

"I live on the fourth floor in the original part of Woodland," she said. "It's one of those rooms with the eaves, and it's really oddly shaped.

"I was very skeptical about ghosts, until I lived here. I've had five deaths in five months in my family, and my best friend said something to me which really made sense to me–she said, 'Maybe you're really sensitive to this realm right now, and maybe that's why you're having a lot of experiences now because you're kind of in tune.'

"I said, 'That *is* kind of cosmic, but it does make sense.

"I've always heard really weird noises coming from one corner of my room. Now I know the knocking of the heaters and all the familiar sounds of Chatham–the 'kalunk' of the old heaters, snow on the roof sliding down, etc. But these sounds were like someone rearranging things and moving around.

"I have dishes and my refrigerator in that corner, and it sounds like someone's sort of touching the dishes and moving things around.

"And no matter how high I crank my heater in that corner, I can't get it hot–it's always freezing."

Heather said while brushing her teeth in her bathroom one day she felt someone tap her on the shoulder. Of course she was alone at the time.

The ghostly roommate has also called Heather's name, and even moved her belongings.

"One day I thought, 'I'm going to test it'," she said. "So I placed my hiking boots in a certain position in my room before I went out for the day, and when I came back later, they were moved! No one else had a key, and nothing

143

else in the room was disturbed."

Heather also had a brush with Woodland's Blue Lady. As she stepped into the dorm's elevator late one evening, the apparition took form in front of her. Shocked, she continued to move into the lift and watched the blue spectral mist dissipate before her eyes. Heather said the experience was brief but disorienting, and she still seemed perturbed by the encounter as she spoke.

The students believe another dorm building, Dillworth, is haunted. "When I lived there I heard a lot of stuff," said Heidi. "I don't know where the access to the area above the top floor is, but there are two round porthole windows up there and a peaked roof. My roommate and I would always hear things up there. It sounded kind of like furniture moving–it was much more than the sound of squirrels or anything like that–this was big, heavy scraping. Nobody lives up there, and we couldn't find a way to get up there, so I don't know who would be up there."

Other students who drifted into the room to catch bits of our conversation concurred with Heidi's story. The mysterious noises in the top of Dillworth are familiar to many students who have lived in the dorm.

The Alumni House is another noisy campus building. According to alumna Alice Adams, those who have slept in the building reported sounds of a party throughout the night. "They said there were ghosts wandering up and down the steps all night," she said.

The spirit which has received the most publicity at Chatham is the ghost of Benedum Hall, a building no longer occupied by the college. Owned by Chatham from 1960 to 1986, the former home of the Benedum family served as a dorm for approximately 30 students.

Students say Claude, the only son of Michael and Sarah Benedum, haunted the hall with his true love Maude, a servant to the Benedums. According to campus legend, the Benedums disapproved of the romance and encouraged their son to enlist in the army in order to separate him from the girl.

Claude joined the Chemical Warfare Corps during World War I, and students said he died at the age of 20 in Benedum Hall after being exposed to poison gas during the war. According to professor Cummins, Claude actually died of pneumonia before he departed for duty.

No one seems to know whether Maude was romantically involved with Claude, or even if she truly existed. It is rumored she died shortly after Claude's death, and students living in the dorm said they heard the moans of the young couple throughout the building. Heidi Clark said she heard that Claude used to pull the covers off girls in Benedum as they slept.

After exhausting the supernatural subject at hand, the group which had assembled in Woodland began to break up and students departed to resume their studies. Heidi, Heather and Lydia hung on, however, and at approximately 11 p.m. we hit the campus to see what we could 'scare up'.

All was quiet as we strode past Dillworth and approached the Andrew W. Mellon Center, another Chatham building with a ghost story. The mansion which now houses administrative offices serves as a social center for the campus.

"The home was a gift to the college in 1940 by Paul Mellon in memory of his illustrious father, Andrew W. Mellon, former U.S. Secretary of the Treasury, founder of the National Gallery of Art in Washington, and one of American's wealthiest men," stated a 1983 Chatham publication about the building.

The Mellons occupied the two and a half story Tudor style home from 1917 to 1921, at which time A.W. Mellon went to Washington.

The brochure outlining the history of the home includes a detailed description of the magnificent structure. "[the home] has a red brick exterior with stone trim and ribbons of leaded glass windows. A limestone balustrade outlines the front terrace. Most of the beautiful stone carvings outside and inside came from George Gray Barnard, who also sold to the Cloisters, the nucleus of the Cloisters Museum in New York.

Almost every room has a marble or carved oak fireplace mantle, such as the elaborate one in the entrance hall imported from Italy. Much of the oak paneling was imported from the Hamilton Palace which stood outside of Glasgow, Scotland."

Many of the thick, wooden arch and doorways in the home appear almost Arthurian in style. Mellon's airy marble solarium makes a striking contrast to the rich, deep tones of the rest of the home–tones which may have helped to perpetuate the stories that ghosts haunt the classic building.

As we approached the back entrance to "Mellon", as students call it, and Heidi reached for the heavy door, a loud clang of another door rang out just a few feet away, sending members of our party scurrying. We later learned the sound was security guard Ray Vock closing the building for the evening. We managed, however, to convince Mr. Vock to take us through the home before he locked it.

While Vock, who has been a security guard at Chatham for 24 years, remains doubtful spirits haunt Mellon, he said he can't deny the unusual experiences he's had in the building.

"It really doesn't bother me, though" he said. "I've worked the midnight shift here for many years. I've heard people say when they first started opening this place up to the students, that's when Andrew started trying to scare them off, but I haven't heard anything lately."

Heather said she's heard reports the third floor of the building is haunted, but most of Mellon's stories center in the building's basement.

The basement houses a two-lane bowling alley and a swimming pool that the *Pittsburgh Press* in 1941 described

146

as "the most luxurious pool in the city."

"About 20 years ago I was down in the bowling alleys with another guard," said Vock. "The pins were up and I threw a ball down the alley and I heard a voice say, 'Get out of here!'

"I turned to the guy I was with and said, 'Did you say that?'

"He said he hadn't, so we thought, 'Did Mr. Mellon say that?!'"

Back up on the first floor of the home, a portrait of Andrew W. Mellon presides authoritatively over the building. Does his spirit still take residence in the Pittsburgh mansion?

Have students merely imagined the hauntings or even concocted the ghost stories? After all, it seems every college must have a ghost.

Many Chatham students believe the campus spirits are not a fabrication. For those who have felt them, it's all part of the Chatham experience.

●

CONCLUSION

Fascination with death–with the unknown– will ensure the endurance of ghost stories. As long as there exists a Pittsburgh and Allegheny County, there will be *ghost stories* of Pittsburgh and Allegheny County.

But do ghosts exist? We must each answer that question in our own way, culling from our experiences and beliefs. For the countless Pittsburghers who shared their supernatural encounters with the author and editor, the answer is affirmative.

As the research deadline for this book approached, it seemed Pittsburgh was suddenly infested with ghost stories.

Many stories the authors uncovered have not been included in this volume, and some which *have* been included were chosen rather arbitrarily–time contraints often led us to the one-ghost-is-as-good-as-the-next philosophy. Not all leads were pursued, and it is certain that some of the region's most interesting tales have been left untouched.

Many of the stories we came across were rather nebulous, and we could't find much but a summary of the tale.

Though no one we spoke with had witnessed the wraith, many told of the Green Man of South Park. The story goes that the park is haunted by a young boy who was struck by lightning and electrocuted there sometime before 1950.

"South Park was a popular place to go parking when I was in high school," said one 46-year-old. "I remember being in my car with a girl when suddenly we heard a thunderous rapping on the window–I was sure it was the

'Green Man!' Turns out it was a motorist in search of a jump start for his car."

North Park also has a story, particularly popular with area grade school children. An ominous green mist is said to descend upon a portion of the road on certain evenings.

Pittsburgh's three rivers harbor many ghost stories, but these, too, seem to be foggy and faint reports.

According to historian and author George Swetnam, clergymen, white horses and red-headed women are dreaded cargo as dictated by the region's river folklore. The Raven, a light-draft boat built in McKeesport in 1852, sailed the Ohio carrying all three harbingers of bad fortune.

The boat sank (as a consequence, some superstitious sailors said), and rivermen later reported the phantom vessel was seen sailing the Ohio each year on the anniversary of the disaster.

Rivermen are not the only superstitious folk in Pittsburgh. Numerous articles have been written about the somewhat unusual beliefs of area coal miners.

The city's turn-of-the-century German South Side community also had its share of superstitions, witches and hexes.

There are the Allegheny Wests–the areas of Pittsburgh and Allegheny County which seem to be supernatural hotbeds, but the stories also spread across the entire region.

The city has given us tales from every neighborhood, every culture–belief in the supernatural is not limited to a portion or a people of Pittsburgh. Without those people, this book would not have been possible.

Author-historian David McCullough speaks fondly of his native Pittsburgh.

"Any writer would love this city," he said. "Any reader would love this city. Stories are here. You can see it ... you can feel it ...it's a haunted place. I'm convinced."

We hope that now, perhaps you, too, are convinced.

●●●

About
the
Author

Beth E. Trapani was between her freshman and sophomore years as a Professional and Creative Writing major at Carnegie Mellon University when she researched and wrote this book.

The Orwigsburg, Schuylkill County, native was the winner of numerous writing awards at Blue Mountain High School and was an editor of the school's newspaper.

As a CMU freshman she attended the Leadership Institute's Broadcast Journalism School in Washington, D.C., and was news director of WRCT-FM, the university radio station.

She later served internships at radio stations T-102-FM and WPPA-AM in Pottsville, WQED-FM in Pittsburgh, and at the Greater Pittsburgh Convention and Visitors Bureau.

Twenty years old at the time of this writing, Beth has been employed by The Princeton Review, where she taught verbal S.A.T. preparation courses; radio station WEEU in Reading, and by the *Reading Eagle* and *Reading Times* in Berks County.

The accomplished writer is also an accomplished rider. Horseback riding and showing is at the top of her list of interests, along with traveling, theater, music, and playing piano.

ACKNOWLEDGEMENTS

ORGANIZATIONS

Caliban Books, Carnegie Mellon University, Homewood Cemetery, Union Dale Cemetery, Pittsburgh History and Landmarks Foundation, Washington County Historical Society, Western Pennsylvania Historical Society, The Carnegie Library of Pittsburgh, Hillman Library, Hunt Library, Shaler Township Library, Blue Mountain High School English Department.

PUBLICATIONS

Allegheny Cemetery: A Romantic Landscape in Pittsburgh by Walter E. Kidney

Devils, Ghosts, and Witches: Occult Folklore in the Upper Ohio Valley by George Swetnam

The Dutchman Died and Other Stories of Pittsburgh's South Side by J. Fred Lissfelt

Haunted Houses by Richard Winer and Nancy Osborn

Life and Architecture in Pittsburgh by James D. Van Trump

More Haunted Houses by Richard Winer and Nancy Osborn Ishmael

Monster on the Allegheny...and Other Lawrenceville Stories by Allen Becer and James and Jude Wudarczyk

Pennsylvania Songs and Legends George Korson, ed.

Pittsburgh, An Urban Portrait by Franklin Toker

Where the Ghosts Are: Favorite Haunted Houses in America and the British Isles by Hans Holzer

Allegheny Journal, The Herald, In Pittsburgh, North Hills News Record, Pittsburgh magazine, *Pittsburgh Post-Gazette, Pittsburgh Press, Sewickley* magazine, *Tribune-Review, Valley News Dispatch*

INDIVIDUALS

Kevin Amos, Rick Antolic, Mary Bonach, Carole Braddock, Wendy Burke, Heather Burtch, Diane Cigan, John DeSantis, Claire DiDominicis, Donald Dorsey, Charlie Gool, Kathy Herrin, Fred Hetzel, Alan Irvine, Susan Javorsky, Janet Kettering, Walter Kidney, Rawena Lynch, Kathy Maron-Wood, Abbey Mendelsson, Sam Minter, Anne New, Rebecca O'Connel, Dick Raugh, Paul Roberts, Roy Sarver, Carolyn Schumacker, David J. Seibold, Patricia A. Stacer, Jean Stimel, George Swetnam, The Trapanis, Jenifer Watkins, Mary Wohleber, Sandy Wright, Frank Zellars.

AND FINALLY...

Thanks to all the nameless individuals who provided support, comfort, aid, direction, and encouragement during the researching, interviewing and writing of this book.

OTHER BOOKS BY
CHARLES J. ADAMS III

(All titles published by Exeter House Books)

Ghost Stories of Berks County (1982)
Ghost Stories of Berks County, Book 2 (1984)
Shipwrecks Near Barnegat Inlet (w/David J. Seibold, 1984)
Legends of Long Beach Island (w/Seibold, 1985)
Shipwrecks off Ocean City (w/Seibold, 1986)
Shipwrecks and Legends 'round Cape May (w/Seibold, 1987)
Ghost Stories of Berks County, Book 3 (w/Gary L. S. Clothier, 1988)
Cape May Ghost Stories (w/Seibold, 1988)
Shipwrecks, Sea Stories and Legends of the Delaware Coast (w/Seibold, 1989)
Ghost Stories of the Delaware Coast (w/Seibold, 1990)
Pocono Ghosts, Legends and Lore (w/Seibold, 1991)
Great Train Wrecks of Eastern Pennsylvania (w/Seibold, 1992)
Ghost Stories of the Lehigh Valley (w/ Seibold, 1993)
Pennsylvania Dutch Country Ghosts, Legends and Lore (1994)

•

FOR A COMPLETE CATALOG OF ALL EXETER
HOUSE BOOKS TITLES, INCLUDING BRIEF
SUMMARIES, PRICES AND ORDERING
INFORMATION, WRITE TO
EXETER HOUSE BOOKS
P.O. BOX 8134
READING, PENNSYLVANIA 19603

•

NOTE: *Reserach has already begun for a possible second volume of Ghost Stories of Pittsburgh and Allegheny County. Anyone with a personal experience or knowledge of a haunting or ghost story in the region is invited to write to the publisher of this book and provide their name, address and contact number. All such responses will be held in strictest confidence.*

PHOTO GALLERY

Students say the Early American Room, one of the University of Pittsburgh's 23 Nationality Classrooms, is haunted. Do ghosts roam the room's hidden loft, reached only by a secret passage?

The Lawrenceville Branch of the Carnegie Library is situated on what was once the Lawrenceville Burying Ground.

The headstone of little Henry Snowden, aged one year, three months, was left behind when the Lawrenceville Burying Ground was moved. Henry's tombstone rests in the library's basement. Does Henry "rest" there, as well?

A ghostly cast of characters is said to roam the stages of The Playhouse on Craft Avenue.

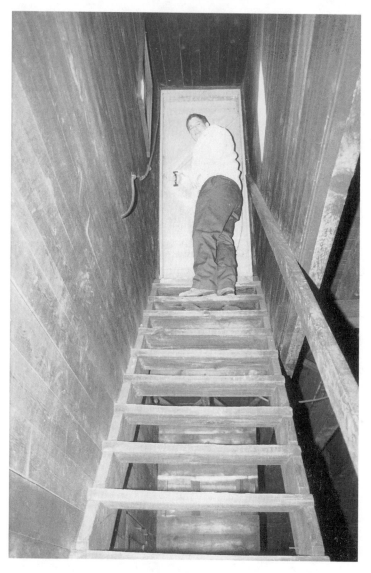

Troy Hill Fire Company Chief Donald Dorsey often takes the steps which lead to the building's hose tower. But, firefighters believe something–or someone–supernatural also roams those stairs.

Do spirits of firefighters long gone still reside in the Troy Hill Fire Company station?

Librarians at the Dormont Library say the spirit of Mary, a particularly popular librarian at one time, remained in the building after her death until her husband, Joe, joined her on her higher plane.

Is it the spirit of "Obie," a past chief, who plagues the members of the Elfinwild Volunteer Fire Company in Glenshaw with paranormal pranks?

The Andrew W. Mellon mansion, a part of Chatham College, has been the scene of ghostly encounters for both students and staff.

162

Is the infamous Blue Lady of Woodland Hall a spectral student at Chatham College?

The apparition of St. Nicholas Croatian Roman Catholic Church in Millvale is one of the county's most prominent ghost stories.

Mural painter Maxo Vanka reported the ghostly figure of a priest garbed in black, making his way down the center aisle at St. Nicholas.

George Swetnam, noted Pittsburgh historian and author, believes the spirit of his home's builder, James B. Kirk, remains in the Glenshaw residence.

Is "The Deacon," the well-intentioned ghost of Allison's Park Depreciation Lands Museum, buried in the cemetery that lies on the museum's grounds?

167

Peter, the spirit of a young boy killed in a fire in the building now occupied by Michael Blaha Flowers, is at times a particularly active little spirit.

David Kornely, owner of Blaha Flowers, has fostered an affection for
his resident wraith.

This mansion at 719 Brighton Road, Allegheny West, has been home to numerous spirits and unusual occurences for several years.

A mysterious large gray lady has been seen peering from the windows of the Thaw Mansion. Has the late Mrs. Thaw, prominent Allegheny West woman in the past, returned to her 930 Lincoln Avenue home?

Students at The Community College of Allegheny County have spied the spectral figure of a woman clinging to the iron fence which surrounds the second floor porch of Byers Hall.

The Byers-Lyon House, now a part of CCAC as Byers Hall, was the scene of the tragic death of Alexander Byer's youngest granddaughter and the suicide of her German nanny in 1902. The spirits of the two females still roam the building, according to many students.